Thank you for your dedication to our students. You are making a difference!

Clark Highsmith

FAMOUS MEN AND WOMEN OF THE CIVIL WAR

by Clark Highsmith

Famous Men and Women of the Civil War
by Clark Highsmith

ISBN 1979153752
EAN-13 978-1979153751

Published in United States by Alacrity Press, 2017
www.alacritypress.com

ALACRITY PRESS

ABOUT THE AUTHOR

Clark Highsmith is a social studies content specialist for a charter school organization in Texas. He is a graduate of Southwest Baptist University and Southwestern Baptist Theological Seminary. An Illinois native, he currently lives in Denton, Texas, with his wife and son. His interests include amateur radio, teaching Sunday School, and watching high school sports. This is Clark's third book and is a follow-up to his other history book, *Famous Men of the Second World War*.

TABLE OF CONTENTS

GENERAL MAP OF THE
UNITED STATES
Showing the area and extent of the
FREE & SLAVE-HOLDING STATES,
and the Territories of the
UNION.

EXPLANATION OF THE COLOURS.

Free-States and Territories coloured Green.
The dark tint above the free settled States and the light tints the Territories.
Slave-holding States coloured Red.
The dark tint above the Slave-importing and also light the Slave exporting states.

Scale of English Miles.

INTRODUCTION

Researching and writing this book has been a joy. It was also a task I could never have completed without the help of others. I first wish to recognize Providence. God reveals again and again that He is in control and is carrying out His will even in tragic human events such as the Civil War. I thank my wife Susan for supporting me and indulging my visits to "empty fields" where obscure battles took place. My son Benjamin inspired me to research and write books about the Famous Men and Women. He also assisted with a technical review of the book.

I thank my editor, Jordan Economidis, for ensuring that my writing is better than it would otherwise have been. Finally, I thank a person I never had the privilege to meet. John Haaren was an early 20th Century educator who wrote a Famous Men series about world history. He helped me to see that history is most interesting when a lesson connects students with the people involved in the events.

The book is generally arranged in chronological order, but each chapter follows the war's course of events from the perspective of a Famous Man or Woman. You may read them in any order or pick and choose as you desire. Let's begin with a quick summary of events leading up to the war.

THE ROAD TO CIVIL WAR

The root causes of the Civil War were in place before America became a nation. Fundamental differences in culture and economics divided the northern and southern states. It would require the lives of over 600,000 people—mostly men—to determine whether the dissimilar cultures would remain one nation or go their separate ways.

During the American Revolution, the states overlooked their differences and worked together. Soon after securing their independence, the states sought a way to strengthen their union without surrendering too much control. The differences were many, but the Founding Fathers recognized slavery as the most divisive issue. Northern states had little use for slavery and thus opposed it. Southern states regarded slavery as essential to their economies.

Most Founding Fathers deplored slavery but believed the institution would eventually die a natural death. John Adams called slavery a "foul contagion." The actions of others were often contradictory. George Washington was known to keep his slaves under strict discipline but provided for their release in his will. Thomas Jefferson, also a slave owner, claimed slavery was a "hideous blot" while also referring to blacks "as incapable as children."

At the 1787 Constitutional Convention, the Framers agreed to end the slave trade but compromised by delaying it for 20 years until 1808. Unfortunately, this had an immediate effect of spurring the slave trade, further expanding slavery. About as many slaves were brought from Africa during this time as were already here.

Invention of the cotton gin in 1794 further encouraged the widespread use of slavery. The gin efficiently removed seeds from cotton. All that was required to take advantage of the gins was a cheap labor force in the form of slaves.

The Missouri Compromise, passed in 1820, only served to define the divide by drawing a line across the continent separating future free and slave states. An attempt by South Carolina to nullify (void or ignore) federal laws in 1833 revealed that some states would go to great lengths to protect their sovereignty.

The pace to civil war quickened in the 1850s. The Fugitive Slave Act compelled northern states to assist in the repulsive practice of capturing escaped slaves. The Kansas-Nebraska Act of 1854 reignited the slavery debate by undoing the Missouri Compromise. It allowed for the possibility of slavery to move into regions where it had been illegal for over 30 years. One immediate consequence was a miniature civil war in the Kansas Territory between pro-slavery "Border Ruffians" and anti-slavery "Jayhawkers."

The *Dred Scott* v. *Sandford* U.S. Supreme Court decision declared that slaves had no rights and that the federal government had no authority to regulate slavery in the territories. Southerners hailed the decision as a victory, while abolitionists decried it.

The John Brown raid in 1859 failed in its bold effort to arm a slave uprising but succeeded in making Brown a martyr in the North. In contrast, Southerners believed northern support of Brown—a murderer who would steal their property—confirmed a conspiracy against their way of life. The anti-slavery expansion policy of President-elect Abraham Lincoln in 1860 was the final insult; the South would attempt to go its own way.

This series of events led to the Civil War between the states. Though millions would participate in the struggle in various ways, only a few would make a name for themselves. This book will introduce you to a number of these intriguing and history-making Famous Men and Women.

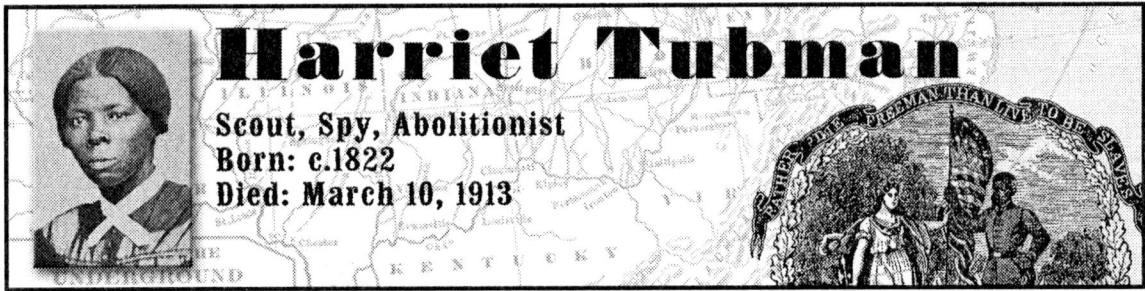

Harriet Tubman

Scout, Spy, Abolitionist
Born: c.1822
Died: March 10, 1913

The first Africans arrived at the Virginia colony in 1619 not as slaves but as indentured servants. Slavery was introduced to the American colonies in 1625 when the Dutch West India Company brought 11 slaves to New Amsterdam (New York). At first, many slaves still enjoyed certain rights. A shortage of slaves led some colonists to enslave Native Americans as well as Africans. Slavery took place in every colony. However, it was much more prevalent in southern colonies that required many laborers.

The morality of slavery was rarely challenged until the latter half of the 18th Century. As white colonists began to seek independence, some began to question the practice of enslaving fellow human beings. Most northern states abolished slavery shortly after the Revolutionary War.

SLAVERY AND THE CONSTITUTION

The Northwest Ordinance of 1787 effectively set the Ohio River as a boundary. Slavery was not allowed in the territories north of the river. When delegates (the Framers) met at the Constitutional Convention in mid-1787, they agreed to end the slave trade, but not until 1808. Another compromise allowed each enslaved person to be counted as three-fifths of a person for purposes of representation. This helped ensure that southern states would have the political power to prevent efforts to end slavery. If the Framers had used a strong hand to deal with slavery, perhaps the Civil War would have never happened.

FROM SLAVERY TO FREEDOM

Harriet Tubman was one of 11 children born to slaves Harriet and Benjamin Ross. Her birth name was Araminta Ross. She was called "Minty" by family and friends.

As a child, Tubman was never taught to read and write. At age four, she cared for her baby brother while her mother worked for their master. At age seven, she was hired out to a neighbor and separated from her family. Minty would cry herself to sleep at night while

This woodcut portrays Harriet as a confident Famous Person.

UNCLE TOM'S CABIN

Few books have had as great an impact as *Uncle Tom's Cabin*. The book was written by an abolitionist, Harriet Beecher Stowe, and first published in book form in 1852. Stowe said, "I would write something that would make this whole nation feel what an accursed thing slavery is." The book was a bestseller. In its first year, 300,000 copies sold in the United States and 1.5 million sold in England. Uncle Tom's Cabin was adapted for the stage and presented in many northern theaters.

The main character of the story is a slave named Tom. Early in the story, Tom rescues a young girl named Eva while on his journey to be sold at the auction block. Eva convinces her father to buy Tom. Eva and Tom develop a strong relationship, learning much from one another. After both Eva and her father pass away, a heart-broken Tom is sold to a wicked plantation owner. Tom eventually dies from a whipping by his master after he refuses to disclose the location of two escaped slaves.

Beecher's book succeeded in uniting support against slavery in the North. Southerners condemned the book as inaccurate. They pointed out that Beecher had never visited the South. The book's influence was felt at every level of society. According to some sources, President Lincoln met Harriet at the White House and said, "So you're the little woman who wrote the book that made this great war."

she lay in front of the fireplace. She once took a lump of sugar without permission. After hiding in a pig pen for four days, she received a beating from the master.

Once Minty was asked by an overseer to help restrain a slave who was leaving the fields without permission. She refused to help. As the slave ran away, the overseer threw a heavy weight. The weight hit Minty instead of the young man, leaving a deep wound. She was forced to return to the fields after two days. Harriet suffered from seizures and headaches for the rest of her life. She would fall asleep at inconvenient times. She also began having dreams that she thought were religious visions.

In 1844, Minty married a free black, John Tubman, and changed her first name to Harriet. She decided to escape in 1849. She later said, "I had reasoned this out in my mind; there was one of two things I had a right to, liberty or death; if I could not have one, I would have the other, for no man should take me alive; I should fight for my liberty as long as my strength lasted, and when the time came for me to go, the Lord would let them take me."

Her husband refused to go with her. Harriet left with her two brothers. The brothers became fearful and turned back. Harriet followed the North Star, eventually reaching Philadelphia. There, she made friends with abolitionists. They helped her find work as a household servant, but Harriet was not content. She resolved to help others escape.

Harriet became a guide, or conductor, on the Underground Railroad. The "railroad" did not use trains or tracks. It was a series of safe houses, or stations, where abolitionists hid slaves. The conductors guided the escaping slaves from station to station.

Tubman's first trip, in 1850, was to rescue her niece, Kessiah, and two children. Harriet's second trip was to rescue her husband. Sadly, Harriet found out that he had remarried a free black and did not want to leave. Harriet made 19 trips, rescuing 300 people, including her 70-year-old parents. She refused to let people turn back, as it

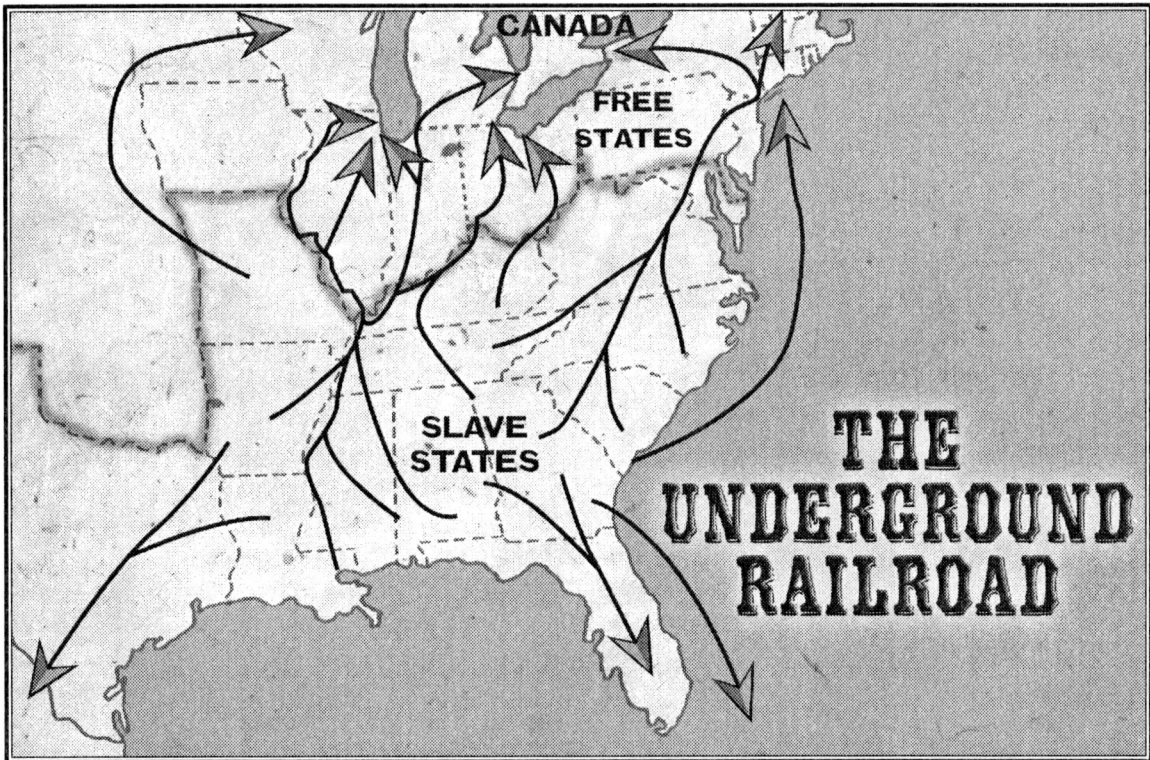

CANADA

FREE STATES

SLAVE STATES

THE UNDERGROUND RAILROAD

would threaten the entire group, and would sings songs to calm them.

Harriet became known as the "Moses of her people." This was based on the biblical story of Moses. God sent him to free the Israelites from slavery in Egypt. Grandma Moses, as she became known, was never captured, and she never lost a passenger.

In 1858, Harriet met John Brown. Brown took a liking to Tubman and helped introduce her to prominent people. Harriet began to speak to groups. During the Civil War, the Governor of Massachusetts recruited Harriet. She served as a cook, nurse, and spy in an occupied part of South Carolina. Tubman recruited former slaves to locate rebel camps and troop movements. The former slaves were more easily able to blend into their surroundings. She helped lead Colonel James Montgomery and Union troops on a raid against suprised Confederates. The raid resulted in the freeing of 800 slaves and the destruction of plantations and fields.

Harriet was never paid for her help. After the war, she made a living by taking in boarders and growing and selling vegetables. With the help of a writer, Harriet published a book, *Scenes in the Life of Harriet Tubman*. The Famous Woman helped raise money for two black schools in South Carolina and even remarried. In 1887, British Queen Victoria sent Tubman a silver medal in honor of Victoria's 60th jubilee. Harriet died in 1913 at the age of 91 and was buried in Fort Hill Cemetery in Auburn, New York.

CONTRIBUTIONS OF BLACK SOLDIERS

The contributions of black soldiers can be traced back to the Revolutionary War. Free black men had even served under a slave owner, George Washington. When the Civil War began, however, the general belief was that blacks did not have a place in either army.

In 1862, Union commanders began to enlist African Americans into segregated units. Enlistment increased sharply after the issue of General Order Number 143 established the Bureau of Colored Troops. Black troops were paid less, served under white officers, and rarely received all the necessary basic equipment. African American units faced an additional menace: Rebels openly threatened to kill any captured black soldiers. The most notable example took place during the Battle of Fort Pillow. The Rebels massacred black Union soldiers attempting to surrender.

The Union formed over 140 black regiments, composed of about 178,000 men, in the final years of the war. The regiment that received the most publicity was the 54th Massachusetts. Organized in March 1863, the 54th was commanded by 26-year-old Colonel Robert Gould Shaw. He belonged to a Boston abolitionist family.

Harriet relaxes during her later years.

LIBRARY OF CONGRESS

This 1890 print depicts the storming of Fort Wagner by the 54th Massachusetts Regiment.

A path wandering through the palmettos at Olustee Battlefield Historic State Park in Florida allows visititors to see a battlefield much different than those found in other states.

The 54th gained national attention after a daring attack against Fort Wagner on Morris Island, South Carolina. Crossing a long strip of beach while under heavy fire, Gould was killed on an enemy parapet while shouting "Forward, 54th!" Though the unit suffered 281 casualties and the attack failed, the bravery of the 54th was widely reported in northern newspapers.

The survivors of the Fort Wagner assault went into Florida to cut beef and salt supply lines and recruit black soldiers. They participated in Florida's largest Civil War engagement, the Battle of Olustee. At Olustee Station, 5000 Confederates awaited the arrival of 5500 Union troops. The Northerners attacked the Confederate positions, leading to a fierce and evenly matched fight. Though much smaller in scale than many other battles, Olustee witnessed the second-highest casualty rate of any Civil War battle. Late in the afternoon, the Union lines broke and retreated from the battlefield. The 54th entered the battle late in the day, preserving the remainder of the Union Army as it escaped.

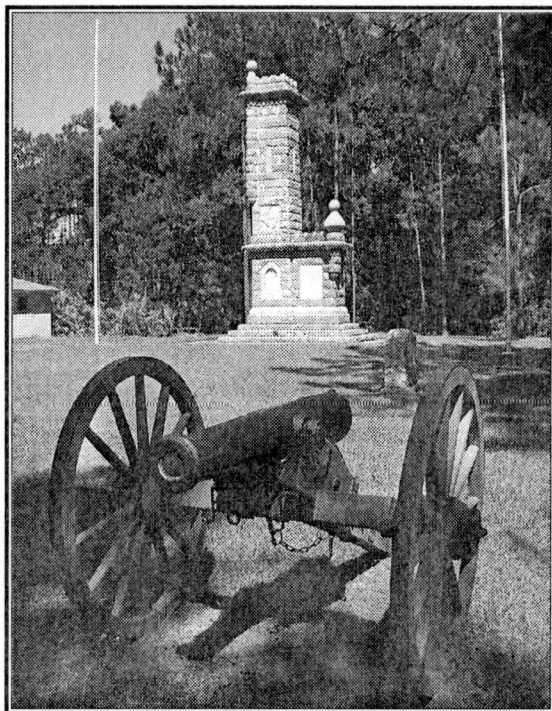

A cannon and monument greet visitors to Olustee Battlefield Historic State Park in Florida.

Abraham Lincoln

16th President of the United States
Born: February 12, 1809
Died: April 15, 1865

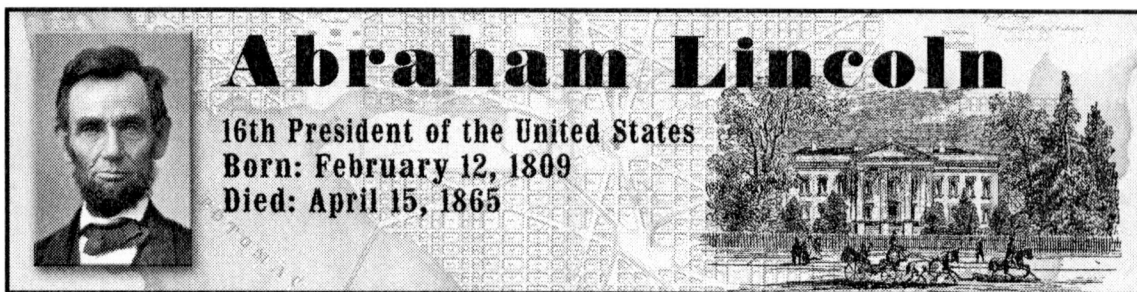

Attempting to conceive how Civil War events would have unfolded without Abraham Lincoln is near impossible. He was the single most influential person in triggering the war and in ending it. For that reason, Lincoln was arguably the most important figure of the Civil War. His election led the southern states to secede. It was Lincoln who willed the Union to prosecute the war to a conclusive end, refusing to compromise on the issue of secession. He forced the nation's hand in ending the institution of slavery.

Lincoln was born in a one-room log cabin on a farm in Hardin County, Kentucky, in 1809. At age seven, his family moved to Indiana. His mother passed away two years later. His father soon married a widow, Sarah Bush. Sarah and Abraham got along well. She recognized Abraham's exceptional mind and personality. Lincoln occasionally attended school but spent most of his days working for his father. He loved to read, borrowing books whenever possible. Lincoln sometimes practiced arithmetic on the back of a shovel using a piece of charcoal.

Lincoln's family moved to Illinois in 1830. The next year, at age 22, Lincoln moved to New Salem, Illinois. Lincoln worked many jobs while living in New Salem. He was a surveyor, clerk, store owner, and postmaster. He loved to give speeches at the New Salem Debating Society. During the Black Hawk War, Lincoln was elected captain of the company from New Salem. During this time, he earned the nickname "Honest Abe." His character showed when he once hiked six miles to refund 6 cents overcharged to a customer.

Lincoln presented a tall, awkward, and often sad appearance. He tended to wear loose, old clothing. His friend and biographer, William Herndon, said that, "melancholy dripped from him as he walked." Lincoln used his unassuming appearance to his advantage. Anyone who underestimated him was surprised by his sharp wit and keen mind. He loved to tell self-belittling stories and could readily dissect an opponent's argument to reveal weaknesses.

Lincoln learned to be a lawyer by reading books. In 1837, he moved to Springfield, Illinois, to practice law. Lincoln refused to represent clients whom he felt were guilty. Every year, he traveled a judicial circuit, interacting with citizens throughout the state. He married Mary Todd in 1842. They had four children, two of whom died in childhood. In 1846, he was elected to the U.S. House of Representatives. After the two-year term, Lincoln returned to Springfield.

In 1856, Lincoln ran for the U.S. Senate. He ran against Stephen Douglas, the incumbent

BENJAMIN HIGHSMITH

The author stands in front of a reproduction of Lincoln's store at New Salem near Springfield, Illinois.

senator who was prominent nationally. Douglas and Lincoln squared off in a series of debates across Illinois. Lincoln lost the election. However, accounts of the debates were published in newspapers around the country. Lincoln thus gained national recognition.

LINCOLN'S ELECTION LEADS TO WAR

The presidential election of 1860 was bitterly contested. Lincoln's supporters helped him secure the Republican nomination. The Democratic Party split, fielding two candidates in John C. Breckinridge and Lincoln's rival, Stephen Douglas. A fourth candidate, John Bell, ran for the Constitutional Party. South Carolina threatened to secede from the Union if Lincoln was elected. Lincoln was not even on the ballot in most southern states. Lincoln won only 39.7%

A LEADER?

Lincoln spent much of the war seeking a general who would take the fight to the Confederates. His first choice, Robert E. Lee, declined and joined the Confederacy. Lincoln then proceeded to work through five generals before finding his man in Ulysses S. Grant.

COMMANDING GENERALS OF THE ARMY OF THE POTOMAC
1. Irvin McDowell (1861)
2. George B. McClellan (1861-1862)
3. Ambrose E. Burnside (1862-1863)
4. Joseph Hooker (1863)
5. George G. Meade (1863-1865)
6. Ulysses S. Grant (1864-1865)

Grant was general-in-chief of all Union armies but headquartered with the Army of the Potomac and directed Meade.

TRIVIA
Lincoln read the Bible every day even though he never officially joined a church. He oftened quoted Bible passages in his speeches.

of the popular vote. However, he won most of the northern states and the all-important Electoral College.

By the time Lincoln took office in March 1861, seven states had already seceded to form the Confederate States of America. After the fall of Fort Sumter, Lincoln declared a blockade of Confederate ports. He also called for 75,000 volunteers to quell the rebellion. This action incited Virginia, Arkansas, North Carolina, and Tennessee to join the Confederacy rather than raise troops to oppose their fellow southern states.

Lincoln was accused by his critics of effectively becoming a dictator. His call for three-year enlistments and the blockade of the Confederacy probably overstepped his constitutional powers. He spent funds on the army without Congressional approval. Problems with southern sympathizers damaging Union railroads led Lincoln to suspend the writ of *habeas corpus*. The constitutional right of *habeas corpus* guaranteed prisoners the right to challenge their confinement in court. Lincoln felt the steps were necessary under the circumstances.

EMANCIPATION PROCLAMATION

It is commonly believed that Lincoln's agenda was to end slavery. While he hated slavery, his only goal was to preserve the Union. He said, "If I could save the Union without freeing any slave I would do it; and if I could save it by freeing all the slaves I would do it; and if I could save it by freeing some and leaving others alone, I would also do that."

A string of military defeats in 1861 and 1862 made it difficult to attract new volunteers for mil-

This Francis Bicknell Carpenter painting depicts Lincoln's reading of his Emancipation Proclamation draft to members of his cabinet. From left: Edwin M. Stanton, secretary of war; Salmon P. Chase, secretary of the treasury; Abraham Lincoln; Gideon Welles, secretary of the navy; Caleb Blood Smith, secretary of the interior; William H. Seward, secretary of state; Montgomery Blair, postmaster general; and Edward Bates, attorney general.

itary service. Lincoln believed that emancipating slaves would provide a new source of manpower for the army. It would also discourage European countries that had already abolished slavery from supporting the South.

Lincoln drafted a document in June 1862. After presenting it to his cabinet, he agreed not to announce the decision until after a Union victory. To do so beforehand might be seen as a desperate act. Lincoln issued the Emancipation Proclamation shortly after the Union victory at Antietam on September 22, 1861.

Technically, the Proclamation did not free a single slave. It only declared that persons held as slaves in rebellious states would be free. The Proclamation did have a powerful effect. Thou-

sands of African Americans enlisted in the Union army. The Proclamation also announced that the Union was not only fighting to preserve the country, but to end human bondage.

GETTYSBURG ADDRESS

In November 1863, Lincoln was invited to speak at the dedication of what is known today as Gettysburg National Cemetery. A year removed from the momentous battle, citizens of Gettysburg created the cemetery out of the necessity to take care of poorly-buried remains of soldiers. Lincoln received an invitation but was not expected to attend.

Lincoln did attend, along with upwards of 20,000 citizens, and sat through a two-hour speech by renowned orator Edward Everett. When his turn came, Lincoln stood up and delivered a two-minute, 271-word speech. The brevity of the speech surprised and disappointed the crowd. Recognized today as brilliant, Lincoln's Gettysburg Address crisply explained his belief that fighting for freedom and equality for all Americans as established in the Declaration of Independence was worth the sacrifice.

THE ELECTION OF 1864

Nearing the end of his first term, Lincoln's prospects for reelection appeared grim. Republicans, afraid that Lincoln would harm other party candidates, openly contemplated nominating alternate candidates. Democrats demonized "Abe the Widowmaker" and appealed to northern racism, labeling his followers "negro-loving, negro-hugging worshipers of old Abe." Calling for an end to the war, even if it meant recognizing Confederate independence, Democrats nominated Lincoln's former general, George McClellan. McClellan supported continuing the war but rejected emancipation as a condition for peace.

In early August 1864, Lincoln believed reelection was unlikely. Admiral Farragut's victory at Mobile Bay, Sheridan's devastating Shenandoah Valley campaign, and Sherman's capture of Atlanta in late summer and early fall energized Lincoln's reelection efforts. Riding strong support from the votes of Union troops, Lincoln won reelection with 55% of the vote.

Congress passed the Thirteenth Amendment on January 31, 1865. The amendment formally abolished slavery. With the end of the Confederacy all but certain, slavery in the United States was finished.

LINCOLN'S ASSASSINATION

Lincoln met with Sherman and Grant onboard his steamship, the *River Queen* in late March 1865. At the meeting, Lincoln explained the conditions of surrender. There was to be leniency, not harsh punishment. He wanted the surrender to begin the healing, not build resentment.

Lincoln toured the front lines during the final days of the war. He visited Richmond just two days after Confederate officials abandoned the city. While in Richmond, several blacks fell to their knees and kissed Lincoln's feet. Lincoln said, "Don't kneel to me, that is not right. You must kneel to God only, and thank Him for the liberty you will hereafter enjoy." He visited the home of George Pickett, whom Lincoln had recommended to West Point

John Wilkes Booth

as a young man. George was away serving in the Confederate Army, but Lincoln consoled his wife and baby boy.

News of Lee's surrender reached Washington on April 10, 1865. Secretary of War, Edwin Stanton, ordered 500 cannons fired in celebration. The next day, Lincoln gave a speech to revelers gathered on the White House lawn. A southern sympathizer and well-known actor, John Wilkes Booth was present. He told a companion, "That's the last speech he will ever make."

T. M. MCALLISTER OF NEW YORK, C.1865-75

Booth was able to approach Lincoln and shoot him in the back of the head.

Executive Mansion,

Washington, _____ , 186__ .

Four score and seven years ago our fathers brought forth, upon this continent, a new nation, conceived in liberty, and dedicated to the proposition that "all men are created equal"

Now we are engaged in a great civil war, testing whether that nation, or any nation so conceived, and so dedicated, can long endure. We are met on a great battle field of that war. We have come to dedicate a portion of it, as a final resting place for those who died here, that the nation might live. This we may, in all propriety do. But, in a larger sense, we can not dedicate — we can not consecrate — we can not hallow, this ground — The brave men, living and dead, who struggled here, have hallowed it, far above our poor power to add or detract. The world will little note, nor long remember what we say here; while it can never forget what they did here.

It is rather for us, the living, to stand here,

Lincoln wrote the notes for his Gettysburg Address while traveling to the cemetery dedication via train.

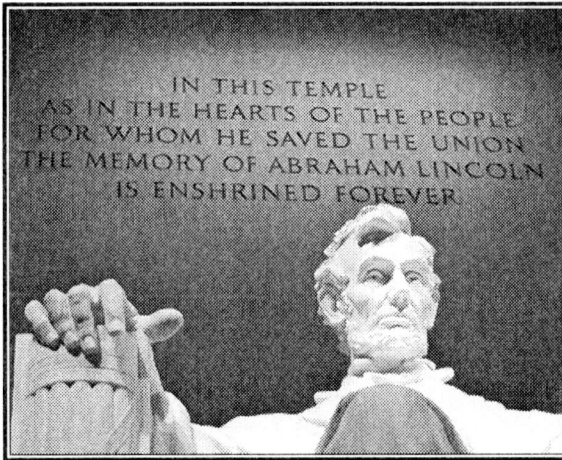

The Lincoln Memorial in Washington, D.C. was completed in 1920.

On April 14th, the Lincolns attended a play, *Our American Cousin* at Ford's Theater in Washington. Familiar with the theater from previous acting engagements, Booth snuck up into Lincoln's box. Lincoln's guard, Detective John F. Parker, had slipped next door to get a drink. Booth pulled out a small pistol and shot the President in the back of the head. Booth broke his leg while jumping from the President's box to the stage. He yelled, "Sic semper tyrannis!" (Death to tyrants!) as he dragged himself outside and escaped on horse. Lincoln passed away the next morning at 7:22 a.m.

The assassination was a part of a bigger conspiracy to take out Union leadership. Lewis Paine was thwarted in his attempt to kill Secretary of State William Seward in bed with a knife. George Atzerodt, assigned to shoot Vice President Andrew Johnson, lost his nerve and did not make the attempt. Booth was found and shot on April 26th in a barn near Port Royal, Virginia. He held no regrets. His dying words were, "Tell mother I die for my country."

The Union's week-long celebration came to a halt as Washington, D.C., prepared for Lincoln's funeral. His body rested in state under the

Painting of Lincoln by George Peter Alexander Healy.

dome of the Capitol building. Spectators lined the tracks to see the train carrying his body back to Illinois. Viewings were held in various cities. Lincoln was buried in Oak Ridge Cemetery in Springfield, Illinois.

The effect of Lincoln's death is difficult to measure. Without Lincoln's single-mindedness, stubbornness, and political genius, the South might have succeeded. Lincoln's contribution toward ending slavery and preserving the Union secures his legacy as one of the greatest Americans. American minister to Britain, Charles Francis Adams, remarked that Lincoln did not possess "any superior genius…" but "…from the beginning to the end, impressed upon the people the conviction of his honesty and fidelity to one great purpose."

Jefferson Finis Davis

President of the Confederate States of America
Born: June 3, 1808
Died: December 6, 1889

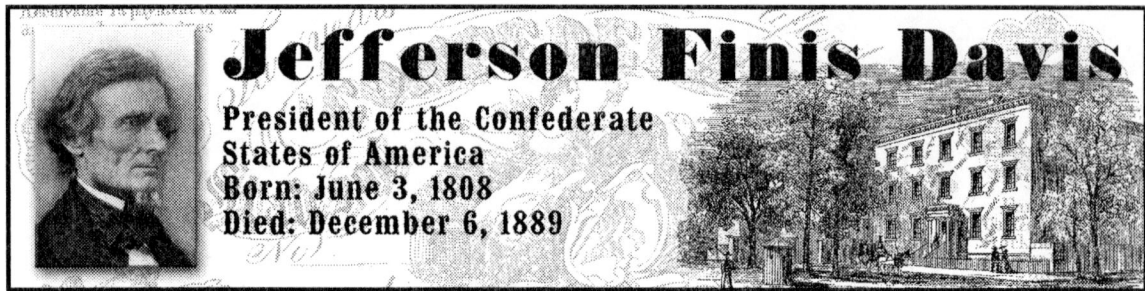

As the first and last President of the Confederacy, Jefferson Finis Davis was the most prominent Rebel leader. Though he was reluctant to accept the position, he embraced the challenge, continuing the fight even after Lee's surrender at Appomattox. Some people characterized him as stubborn and overconfident. Others—especially Southerners—revered Davis as a man of high character and energy.

Like his Northern counterpart, Abraham Lincoln, Davis was born in a log cabin in Kentucky. He was the youngest of 10 children. His father had fought in the Revolutionary War. Davis' family moved to the small town of Woodville along the Mississippi River in southwest Mississippi. His family named its estate Rosemont.

Jefferson returned to Kentucky to attend a private school at age eight. At fifteen, he attended Transylvania College, excelling as an honor student. The death of Davis' father left the family in poverty. Lacking oney, Jefferson decided to attend West Point as it offered free tuition. Davis did well academically but was often cited for behavior such as messiness and missing roll call. He graduated 23rd out of 33 cadets in his class. His first assignment was at Jefferson Barracks near St. Louis. He fought in the Black Hawk War, helping with the capture of Chief Black Hawk.

In 1835, Davis married Sarah Knox "Knoxie" Taylor, daughter of future U.S. President Zachary Taylor. They moved onto family land, which he named Brierfield. Three months after their marriage, Jefferson and Sarah each contracted malaria. Jefferson recovered, but Sarah died. Heartbroken by the loss of his wife, Davis threw himself into learning how to make his plantation prosperous.

Brierfield, like other large southern plantations, required the labor of many slaves. Davis banned his overseers from using corporal punishment. He allowed his slaves to establish a "court" in which they heard cases and passed sentence themselves.

ENTRY INTO POLITICS

Davis' skill as a powerful orator led to his involvement in politics. He was elected to the U.S. House of Representatives at age 38, and he remarried the same year. He was wounded in the foot at the Battle of Buena Vista during the Mexican-American War while serving as a Colonel of Mississippi Volunteers. He turned down an offer to become brigadier general, instead accepting Mississippi's vacant Senate seat.

President Franklin Pierce selected Davis to serve as Secretary of War in 1853. Davis was responsible for one of the stranger events in American history. In 1856, Davis arranged for the purchase of 100 camels from Egypt to be used by the U.S. Army in the Southwest. While the camels were effective, they fell out of use during the Civil

TRIVIA

Confederate President Jefferson F. Davis is not to be confused with Union General Jefferson C. Davis. During the war, Jefferson C. Davis murdered another Union general after a personal argument. Davis avoided prosecution because the need for qualified leaders for an imminent campaign took precedence.

War and reverted to the wild. The last camel was sighted in 1941 near Douglas, Texas.

BLEEDING KANSAS

In 1854, the Kansas-Nebraska Act opened up new territories to settlers. Illinois Senator Stephen A. Douglas advocated the idea of popular sovereignty, under which the citizens of the new territories would decide whether to allow slavery. Senator Jefferson Davis helped organize Democratic support for the Kansas-Nebraska Act.

Passage of the Act caused great upheaval. It undid the Missouri Compromise that had prevented slavery north of the 36° 30′ parallel. The Act opened the possibility of slavery in places where it had not been allowed for over 30 years.

Many settlers entered the Kansas Territory seeking land and a better life. They were joined by abolitionists and pro-slavery supporters who rushed to Kansas just to influence the formation of the territorial government. Abolitionist settlers were known as Jayhawkers. Border ruffians were Missouri residents who hated Yankee abolitionists and the idea of free blacks living nearby. They crossed into Kansas, voted illegally, and engaged in violence meant to intimidate residents. Border ruffians flocked to the polls during the election

AUTHOR PHOTO

Busts of Jefferson Davis and his second wife, Varina, are on display at the Vicksburg County Courthouse.

The violence of Bleeding Kansas spilled over into the U.S. Senate in 1856. South Carolina Congressman Preston Brooks nearly killed Massachusetts Senator Charles Sumner after his speech denouncing the possibility of slavery in Kansas

WHAT'S IN A NAME?

The name by which one referred to the Civil War often revealed one's point of view.

- Civil War
- The War Between the States—a favorite name in the South
- War for the Union
- The Late Unpleasantness
- War for Southern Independence
- The Brothers' War
- North vs. South
- The War of the Rebellion or simply The Rebellion — Since the United States did not recognize the Confederacy, war was technically impossible—it was a rebellion.

to establish a territorial government. Due to over half of the votes being fraudulent, a pro-slavery government was elected.

The Jayhawkers attempted to create their own constitution and government. This led to a violent in-state civil war known as Bleeding Kansas. The violence even reached Washington, D.C., in 1856. South Carolina Congressman Preston Brooks attacked, and almost killed, Massachusetts Congressman Charles Sumner on the floor of the U.S. Senate.

John Brown was one of the prominent leaders of the Jayhawkers. Unlike most abolitionists, Brown saw violence as a good way to end slavery. In one tragic incident that foreshadowed future violence, Brown, his sons, and his followers attacked anti-slavery settlers at Potawatomi. They stabbed and hacked five men to death with swords.

JOHN BROWN RAID

Brown was responsible for one of the more explosive acts leading up to the Civil War. He returned to the East from Bleeding Kansas in order to raise money to fund an insurrection. On Sunday, October 16, 1859, Brown led a group of about 20 followers across the Potomac River from Maryland to seize the federal arsenal at Harpers Ferry, Virginia. They planned to take arsenal guns, flee to the mountains, and call on slaves to join him in rebellion. Instead, the group was surrounded by local militia.

U.S. Army Colonel Robert E. Lee led marines in storming the arsenal. During the assault, 17 people died, including Brown's two sons and eight of his other followers. Brown was tried and convicted of murder and treason. Shortly before his execution on December 2nd, Brown wrote, "I, John Brown, am now quite certain that the crimes of this guilty land will never be purged away but with

John Brown

NATIONAL ARCHIVES AND RECORDS

President of the Confederate States of America Jefferson Davis

blood." Abolitionists viewed him as a martyr who gave his life for a just cause. Southerners were sickened at the thought of a long-held fear almost coming true—vengeful slaves rising in rebellion. After John Brown's raid, reconciliation between North and South became almost impossible.

ELECTION AND FORT SUMTER

After the election of Abraham Lincoln as President, pro-slavery supporters colorfully described as "fire-eaters" made good on their promise to leave the Union. South Carolina seceded first on December 20, 1860. Mississippi, Alabama, Florida, Georgia, Louisiana, and Texas quickly followed.

On February 10, 1861, Davis received a telegram announcing that the new Confederate government had elected him President. Davis did not take it well. His wife Varina said, "After a few minutes' painful silence he told me, as a man might speak of a sentence of death." He accepted reluctantly. Davis stated that the Confederacy would "seek no conquest, no aggrandizement, no concession of any kind from the States with which we were lately confederated; all we ask is to be left alone."

Tossing aside his initial reservations, Davis embraced his new job. He wrote a constant flow of letters and involved himself in every detail. Under his leadership, the Confederate government swelled to 70,000 employees.

The southern states' first military move was to seize federal property and arsenals. Only Forts Sumter in South Carolina and Pickens in Florida remained under Union control at the time of Lincoln's inauguration. Major Robert Anderson was in charge of Sumter, a pentagon-shaped fort protected by 12-foot thick walls that stood 40 feet high.

President Lincoln had to make the difficult decision of whether to reinforce Fort Sumter. Doing so would likely start a conflict. Lincoln informed South Carolina that he was sending provisions, but no reinforcements. Anderson rejected all calls to surrender On April 11th, Confederate guns opened up on Sumter by order of Confederate General P.G.T. Beauregard. A lack of ammunition limited the Union's ability to respond. Anderson surrendered after 34 hours of bombardment. Amazingly, the only five casualties were from a Union cannon that exploded. Private Daniel Hough became the first man to die in the war.

Major Robert Anderson

After the attack, Lincoln called up 75,000 militia. Lincoln's action encouraged North Carolina, Virginia, Arkansas, and Tennessee to join the Confederacy. After Virginia seceded, the Confederate capital was moved from Montgomery, Alabama to Richmond, Virginia. Davis and his family lived in the grand, three-story Richmond White House.

The Confederate White House was a rather ordinary three-story building in Richmond, Virginia.

The Confederate Flag flies over Fort Sumter after Anderson's surrender.

The Confederacy faced many disadvantages, lacking manpower, industrial capacity, and international recognition. The number of soldiers peaked in 1863. At that time, hunger and loss of manpower began to be an issue. Efforts to switch from cash to food crops faltered, and Union invasions destroyed fields and stores of crops. Industrial establishments were put under military authority. Many European countries sympathized with the South, but the issue of slavery could not be overcome. No other nation officially recognized the Confederacy. One advantage that the South did hold was that it did not have to win the war, but only had not to lose.

As the war progressed, the Confederates abandoned their states' rights ideals. The increasingly centralized government used impressment and drafts to prop up the military. Laws suspended *habeas corpus* and created a tax to confiscate property. Davis employed a socialist economy run from the top down by the War Department. Weeks before the war ended, a desperate Confederate Congress approved limited emancipation and enrollment of slaves into the army.

SYMBOL OF THE LOST CAUSE

While attending church on April 2, 1865, Davis received a telegram from Lee that he was abandoning the Petersburg defenses. Union soldiers would soon enter Richmond. Davis and his officials moved the government southward. The last war council was held in Abbeville, South Carolina on May 2nd. Meeting with Secretary of War John C. Breckinridge and General Braxton Bragg, Davis talked about continuing the war from west of the Mississippi. Davis was captured by northern forces on May 10th. He spent two years in prison at Fort Monroe without a trial.

Davis continued to defend the South after his release. He published *The Rise and Fall of the Confederate Government*, a 1200-page defense of secession and the war. Davis lived his final days at Beauvoir, a beachfront home on the Mississippi Gulf Coast. The home, badly damaged by Hurricane Katrina in 2005, serves today as a Presidential library for Davis. Davis died in 1889 at the age of 81 in New Orleans. Thousands of supporters attended his funeral procession.

Jefferson Davis' legacy is that he was a symbol of the Lost Cause. Ridiculed by the northern press and admired by Southern sympathisers, he remains one of the most widely-recognized men of the Civil War.

CHRISTOPHER MARDORF/FEMA

Jefferson Davis lived out his final days at Beauvoir in Biloxi, Mississippi.

FLAGS OF THE CONFEDERACY

STARS AND BARS – 7 STARS

The Stars and Bars flag was adopted on March 4, 1861. It featured two red bars and seven white stars against a blue canton (upper left corner box). The stars represented the original seven states that formed the Confederacy.

STARS AND BARS – 13 STARS

The Stars and Bars evolved as new states joined the Confederacy. This version features 13 stars in the canton under the fanciful assumption that Confederate shadow governments in border states Missouri and Kentucky were legitimate.

THE STAINLESS BANNER

Many Rebels felt that the Stars and Bars too closely resembled the flag of the United States. The Stainless Banner flag was adopted on May 1, 1863. It featured a white field with the battle flag of the Army of Northern Virginia as the canton.

CONFEDERATE FLAG 1865

The white field of the Stainless Banner proved troublesome. On the battlefield it resembled a flag of truce or surrender. On March 4, 1865, a red bar was added to the right side of the flag. The flag was shortlived as the war drew to a close in the months after it was adopted.

P.G.T. Beauregard

Confederate General
Born: May 28, 1818
Died: February 20, 1893

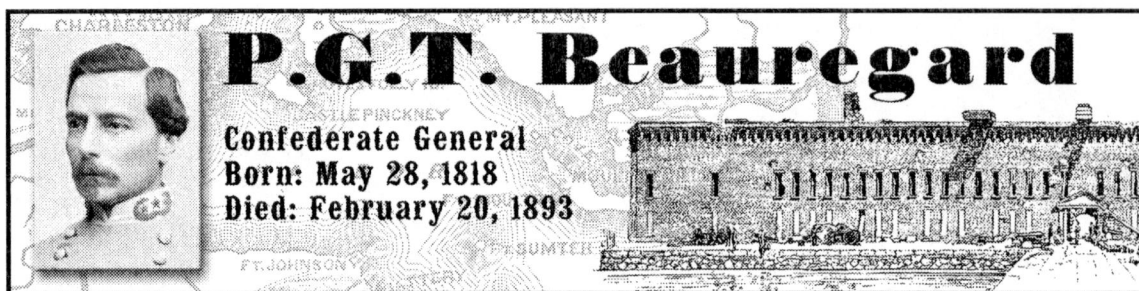

Difficult times define leaders. Weak leaders are sharply criticized. Strong, competent leadership can quickly elevate an obscure person into a legend. Pierre Gustave Toutant Beauregard, better known as P.G.T. Beauregard, was a leader who emerged as one of the South's most prominent leaders in the early stages of the war.

Beauregard was born near New Orleans to a Creole family of French, Italian, and Welsh descent. He was an exceptional cadet at West Point, graduating second out of 48 cadets in 1838. The army employed his engineering skills in construction and drainage projects along the Mississippi River and the coast. During the Mexican-American War he was cited twice for bravery after being twice wounded.

Beauregard was not very tall but was a man of style. He dressed well and used proper manners. His polished manners earned him a reputation as the ideal of the southern gentleman officer. However, some people viewed him as pompous. They made fun of his height by calling him "Little Napoleon" and "Little Creole."

In January 1861, P.G.T. was placed in charge of West Point as superintendent. The next month, he was fired after announcing that he would follow his state if it seceded. After his dismissal, he resigned from the U.S. Army and offered his services to the Confederacy.

Pierre was sent to Charleston where he used his engineering skills to oversee the siege of Fort

NATIONAL PARK SERVICE

Pierre Gustave Toutant Beauregard poses in his Confederate general's uniform.

THE PHOTOGRAPHIC HISTORY OF THE CIVIL WAR

Beauregard rallied his troops near the Henry House Hill during the First Battle of Bull Run.

S.S. BALTIC. OFF SANDY HOOK APR. EIGHTEENTH. TEN THIRTY A.M. .VIA

NEW YORK. . HON. S. CAMERON. SECY. WAR. WASHN. HAVING DEFENDED

FORT SUMTER FOR THIRTY FOUR HOURS UNTIL THE QUARTERS WERE EN

TIRELY BURNED THE MAIN GATES DESTROYED BY FIRE. THE GORGE WALLS

SERIOUSLY INJURED. THE MAGAZINE SURROUNDED BY FLAMES AND ITS

DOOR CLOSED FROM THE EFFECTS OF HEAT .FOUR BARRELLS AND THREE

CARTRIDGES OF POWDER ONLY BEING AVAILABLE AND NO PROVISIONS

REMAINING BUT PORK. I ACCEPTED TERMS OF EVACUATION OFFERED BY

GENERAL BEAUREGARD BEING ON SAME OFFERED BY HIM ON THE ELEV

ENTH INST. PRIOR TO THE COMMENCEMENT OF HOSTILITIES AND MARCHED

OUT OF THE FORT SUNDAY AFTERNOON THE FOURTEENTH INST. WITH

COLORS FLYING AND DRUMS BEATING. BRINGING AWAY COMPANY AND

PRIVATE PROPERTY AND SALUTING MY FLAG WITH FIFTY GUNS. ROBERT

ANDERSON. MAJOR FIRST ARTILLERY. COMMANDING.

Major Robert Anderson sent this telegram to his superiors after surrendering Fort Sumter to General P.G.T. Beauregard.

Sumter. The Civil War began when he ordered a bombardment of the fort. The capture of Fort Sumter elevated Beauregard to a status as a southern hero. However, one of the few southerners who did not admire him was President Jefferson Davis. Despite his misgivings, Davis assigned Beauregard to work under Joseph E. Johnston preparing defenses in northern Virginia.

Beauregard played an important role in the first major infantry struggle of the war, the Battle of First Bull Run. Pressured by President Lincoln and northern politicians, General Irvin McDowell moved his inexperienced forces against Beauregard's positions along Bull Run Creek near Manassas Junction. Beauregard rallied soldiers near the Henry House Hill where the fighting was fiercest. Despite winning the battle, Beauregard was criticized for not capitalizing on the Union's retreat

BORDER STATES

Military leaders on both sides struggled to organize orderly fighting units in the early days of the war. Meanwhile, another war was being waged for the loyalty of the border states. Missouri, Kentucky, Maryland, Delaware, and the region of Virginia that would become West Virginia did not clearly lean towards the North or South. Whichever side earned the allegiance of the border states would gain a clear advantage.

DELAWARE

Delaware was the smallest of the border states. While it allowed slavery, there were only about 1800 slaves. The state never seriously threatened to join the South and remained loyal to the Union.

MARYLAND

Maryland surrounded Washington, D.C. on three sides. Therefore, President Lincoln knew that holding Maryland was critical. However, the southern and coastal parts of Maryland strongly

WHO'S WHO?

The two opposing sides during the Civil War went by many names.

THE CONFEDERATE STATES
OF AMERICA
South
Gray
the Confederates
Johnny Reb
Rebels

THE UNITED STATES
OF AMERICA
North
Blue
the Union
Billy Yank
Federals

identified with Virginia. Marylanders in these areas wanted the state to join the Confederacy.

Some of the first casualties of war took place in Baltimore on April 6, 1861. Union troops passing through the city were attacked by a pro-South mob. The violence spread as southern sympathizers destroyed railroad bridges and telegraph lines. For a short time, the fate of Washington, D.C., was quite uncertain. The Maryland legislature only fueled the violence by refusing to choose a side.

Lincoln sent troops to occupy Maryland, end the violence, and restore lines of communication. The President authorized the arrest of Maryland officials suspected of plotting against the Union. Many were held without the right of habeus corpus, an action justified as a wartime necessity. Union supporters and the occupying troops prevented Maryland from joining the Confederacy.

MISSOURI

Missouri was another border state that experienced violence. The governor, Claiborne F. Jackson, persuaded the Democratically-controlled legislature to call a secession convention. On February 18, 1861, Missouri voters rebuked Claiborne by electing delegates to the convention who did not favor immediate secession. Sterling Price was elected as the presiding officer. The convention voted against secession, but also made clear that itdid not support the North's effort to coerce the South.

Missouri was the site of the first major battle in the western theater, the Battle of Wilson's Creek, in August 1861. The outcome ensured that the state would nominally remain with the Union. Confederate supporters formed a shadow government in October 1861 with Jackson as governor. The shadow government had little influence and was soon driven from the state. However, it did send representatives to the Confederate Congress and was represented by a star on Beauregard's Confederate battle flag.

P.G.T. Beauregard designed the battle flag of Army of Northern Virginia.

KENTUCKY

The issue of secession bitterly divided Kentucky. This state was also the most influential of the border states. Lincoln said, "I think to lose Kentucky is nearly the same as to lose the whole game. Kentucky gone, we cannot hold Missouri, nor Maryland. These all against us, and the job on our hands is too large for us."

Governor Beriah Magoffin called the Kentucky legislature into session in order to call a state convention. Indecision and disagreements led the legislature to adjourn without calling a convention, instead claiming neutrality. Northerners viewed neutrality as little different than secession.

Lincoln knew keeping Kentucky from joining the Confederacy would require diplomacy. He declared that he had the right to send troops into Kentucky, but assured Kentucky he would not do so if the state "...made no demonstration of force against the United States..." In the early days of the war, supplies flowed to Tennessee through Kentucky, but Lincoln hesitated to intervene. In the 1861 summer state elections, Kentucky voters moved the state firmly into Union hands. Kentucky remained in the Union even as many Kentuckians enlisted to fight with Southern military units.

SHILOH AND BEYOND

During the First Battle of Bull Run, Beauregard and other leaders realized that the Confederacy's "Stars and Bars" flag was easily confused with the the Union's "Stars and Stripes." In response, Beauregard designed a flag that became the battle flag of North Virginia. The battle flag was never officially the flag of the Confederacy. However, it became synonymous with the Confederacy and an enduring, but controversial, symbol of the South.

Beauregard's success at Bull Run increased his popularity among southerners. Davis promoted him to full general rather than risk angering Beauregard's many admirers. Beauregard joined the Army of Tennessee under Albert Sydney

Johnston. He drafted the battle plans for the attack against Ulysses S. Grant's troops near Shiloh church in southern Tennessee. When Johnston was killed during the battle, overall command fell to Beauregard. He was criticized for not pressing the attack when Grant's troops were in total confusion on the first day of battle.

When Union reinforcements arrived on the second day at Shiloh, Beauregard retreated to Corinth, Mississippi. Realizing he was greatly outnumbered and could not hold the vital rail junction, Beauregard planned a withdrawal. He had logs painted black to look like cannons. Troops were told to cheer empty railcars entering the city in order to convince Union soldiers that reinforcements were arriving. The withdrawal was well-executed but angered President Davis. Shortly after evacuating Corinth, Beauregard became ill. Davis used the illness as an excuse to remove him from command and appoint Braxton Bragg in his place.

After recovering, Beauregard took the low-profile job of preparing defenses for the Georgia and South Carolina coasts. In April 1863, he prevented Charleston from falling into Union hands by repelling several land and naval attacks.

DEFENDING RICHMOND

In 1864, Beauregard joined Robert E. Lee in Virginia. He reinforced Richmond's defenses, including Drewry's Bluff, a fort on a 90-foot bluff seven miles from Richmond on the James River. A May 1864 attack against Drewry's Bluff by Benjamin Butler captured the outer portion of the fort. Beauregard led a counterattack driving out Butler's Union soldiers. Beauregard then moved to the Carolinas where he ended the war alongside Joseph E. Johnston.

After the war, Beauregard served as a railroad president in New Orleans and in the state government. His wartime efforts earned him a high reputation abroad. Romania and Egypt asked him to lead their armies. He declined both offers. In his later days, Beauregard wrote books and articles about the Civil War and military matters. He died in 1893 and was buried in the tomb of the Army of Tennessee in a New Orleans cemetery.

Though his influence waned during the course of the war, Beauregard's place among the Famous Men is assured. He led the South to important victories during the early days of the war and faithfully served for the duration.

LIBRARY OF CONGRESS

Drewery's Bluff as it appeared during the Civil War

Winfield Scott

Union General
Born: June 13, 1786
Died: May 29, 1866

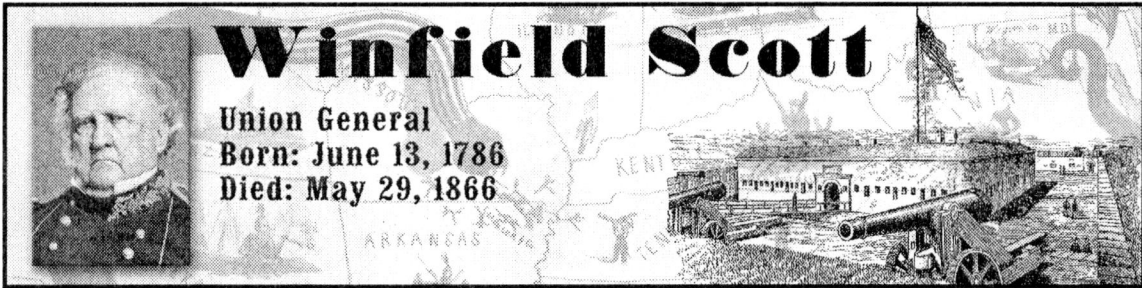

Winfield Scott was born near Petersburg, Virginia one year before delegates gathered in Philadelphia to write the Constitution of the United States. The son of a Revolutionary War veteran, Scott embarked on a brief law career after attending William & Mary College.

Scott found his true calling when he joined a U.S. Army cavalry unit in 1807. Thus began a 54-year career. He earned a commission in artillery but was frustrated by conflicts with superior officers. While serving in New Orleans in 1810, he accused General James Wilkinson of misconduct. Scott was court-martialed even though the accusations proved true.

Winfield Scott
War of 1812

After one year, he returned to duty as a lieutenant colonel and participated in the invasion of Canada during the War of 1812. At one point, he was captured by the British and held for three months. During the war he realized that the army was poorly trained and led. He would soon have the chance to do something about it.

In 1814, Scott was promoted to Major General. He initiated reforms, organized formal training, and wrote a standard drill book. He recruited and promoted officers based on merit rather than politics or social standing. He visited Europe to study training methods. His attention to detail and protocol earned him the nickname "Old Fuss and Feathers."

Scott gained a reputation as an expert negotiator with Indians and with the British in border disputes. In 1841, Scott was given control of the

U.S. soldiers cheer Winfield Scott after the Battle of Cerro Gordo during the Mexican-American War.

Robert Walter Weir painted this portrait of Scott in 1855.

This imaginative 1861 cartoon lampoons Scott's Anaconda Plan while mocking the Confederate states.

entire U.S. Army. When the Mexican-American War began in 1846, Scott led an expeditionary force from Veracruz inland to Mexico City. Despite facing Mexican forces with superior numbers, Scott was able to take Mexico City, allowing the United States to dictate favorable terms in the Treaty of Guadalupe Hidalgo. The Duke of Wellington called Scott's campaign the most well-executed in the modern era.

In 1852, Scott ran unsuccessfully for president as a Whig, losing to Democrat Franklin Pierce. When the Civil War began, the "father of the U.S. Army" had been serving his country for over 50 years. He decided to remain with the Union rather than his native Virginia. Scott said, "I have served my country, under the flag of the Union, for more than 50 years, and so long as God permits me to live, I will defend that flag with my sword, even if my native state assails it."

ANACONDA PLAN

Scott was too old and overweight to lead an army in battle. However, his plan was to bring the South to its knees without direct military confrontation. He envisioned a series of strong camps along state borders and a blockade of Confederate ports and rivers. The public ridiculed the idea and demanded an immediate invasion of the

South. George McClellan remarked that the plan on paper looked like a boa constrictor. Newspapers called it the Anaconda Plan.

Continuing criticism drove Scott to retire in November 1861. As the war raged, Scott wrote his memoirs and revisited Europe. Scott died on May 29, 1866 at West Point, New York and was buried in the West Point cemetery.

Scott's Anaconda Plan was fully embraced one year into the war. Confederate ports were blockaded, preventing international trade. Union troops pushed down the Mississippi River from Cairo, Illinois while also working up the Cumberland and Tennessee rivers.

In early 1862, Ulysses S. Grant and the Union river fleet captured Forts Henry and Donelson on the Cumberland and Tennessee rivers. This paved the way for the capture of Nashville. In May 1862, Flag Officer David Farragut and Major General Benjamin C. Butler captured New Orleans. The fall of Vicksburg in July 1863 gave the Union control of the Mississippi River. The Confederacy was cut in half. Though Scott never took to the field, his Anaconda Plan was a key in winning the war by depriving the South of goods and weapons.

IRONCLADS

Implementing the Anaconda Plan was an ambitious undertaking. The job was made easier by the rapid advancement of naval technology. The Civil War witnessed the completion of a technological revolution that began with the invention of the steam engine. The introduction of ironclads marked the

LIBRARY OF CONGRESS

The USS *Monitor* and CSS *Virginia* (*Merrimack*) engage at close range during the Battle of Hampton Roads on March 9, 1862.

beginning of the end of wooden warships that had fought since the dawn of naval warfare.

Sailors had known for centuries that wooden ships were vulnerable to metal projectiles. Korean naval commander Yi Sun-shin experimented with "turtle ships" protected by iron during the 16th Century. However, it was the invention of the steam engine, and a desire to protect it, that led to the ironclads of the Civil War.

In early 1861, the Norfolk Naval Yard in Virginia fell into Confederate hands. The Rebels raised the USS *Merrimack*, a ship that retreating Union workers had burned to the waterline.

The Rebels rebuilt the ship, layering two-inch metal plates on the exterior to create four inches of armor. They added six nine-inch smoothbore cannons, four rifled guns, and a cast-iron ram. The heavy ship could only manage four knots per hour with its old engines that had been condemned by the Union Navy. It was also difficult to steer. The odd-looking ship was derisively called a floating barn roof. It was launched on March 5, 1862 and was renamed CSS *Virginia*.

The Union was aware of the *Virginia* and feared that a single ironclad could allow shipping to pass through the blockade. The Union responded with its own ship, the USS *Monitor*. The *Monitor* had a flat deck, four and a half inches of iron plating, and a 140-ton revolving turret housing two 11-inch smoothbore cannons.

Naval engineer John Ericsson and his crew built the ship in less than 100 days. The *Monitor* was capable of six knots and was lighter, smaller, and more maneuverable than the Virginia. It too was given a derisive nickname as the "cheese box on a raft."

On March 8, 1862, the *Virginia* under command of Captain Franklin Buchanan, sallied forth into Hampton Roads waterway. It rammed and sank the 30-gun USS *Cumberland* before forcing the 50-gun USS *Congress* and the 44-gun USS *Minnesota* to run aground. Buchanan's brother onboard the *Congress* was killed when its

Franklin Buchanan

powder magazine exploded. The *Virginia* was hit 98 times, but no shells penetrated the hull.

Over 240 Union sailors were killed during the battle while only two Rebel sailors died. Buchanan was injured by a musket ball and did not participate the next day. It was the worst U.S. naval defeat until Pearl Harbor in 1941. The Union moved the *Monitor* to Hampton Roads from New York overnight,

The next morning, the *Virginia* sallied out again and was met by the *Monitor*. For over two hours, the two ships pelted one another with cannonballs and shells. The battle paused long enough for the Union ship to withdraw and load more ammunition. The battle finally ended when the *Virginia* targeted the *Monitor's* turret. Captain John L. Worden was blinded when a shot exploded

John Worden

through his observation slot. The *Monitor* withdrew, as did the *Virginia*.

The USS *Monitor* sinks in the Atlantic Ocean while the USS *Rhode Island* looks on.

The *Virginia* never ventured out again. It was intentionally sunk before Union troops could capture it during the Peninsula Campaign. In May 1862, the *Monitor* led a flotilla of five boats up the James River. The flotilla was stopped at Drewry's Bluff because the *Monitor* could not elevate its guns enough to attack positions on the 90-foot high bluff. The *Monitor* sank on December 31, 1862 when it encountered strong winds off the coast of Cape Hatteras, North Carolina.

CSS HUNLEY

Ironclads were just one major naval innovation during the war. Thanks to the innovative ideas of Horace L. Hunley, the Confederates were the first to ever use a submarine to sink an enemy ship.

Hunley's ship was more like a small half-submerged, tube-shaped boat. P.G.T. Beauregard referred to it as the "fish-torpedo." Serving on the *Hunley* required true bravery. It sank three times during trials, killing most of the three crews including Hunley during the second attempt.

On February 17, 1864, a fourth crew of eight men hand-cranked the *Hunley* into Charleston Bay. The *Hunley* successfully rammed the USS *Housatonic* and deployed a 135-pound mine in the ship's interior. As the *Hunley* backed away, a great explosion rocked and sank the *Housatonic*. The *Hunley* failed to return to its base. It vanished without a trace. Researchers believe that the shock wave from the explosion instantly killed the *Hunley's* sailors.

The *Hunley* was located on the bed of Charleston Bay in 1995 and was raised in 2000. It is housed at the Warren Lasch Conservation Center in North Charleston, South Carolina where it is being restored.

AMERICAN CIVIL WAR MUSEUM

Conrad Wise Chapman created this painting of the *H.L. Hunley* torpedo boat (submarine) in December, 1863.

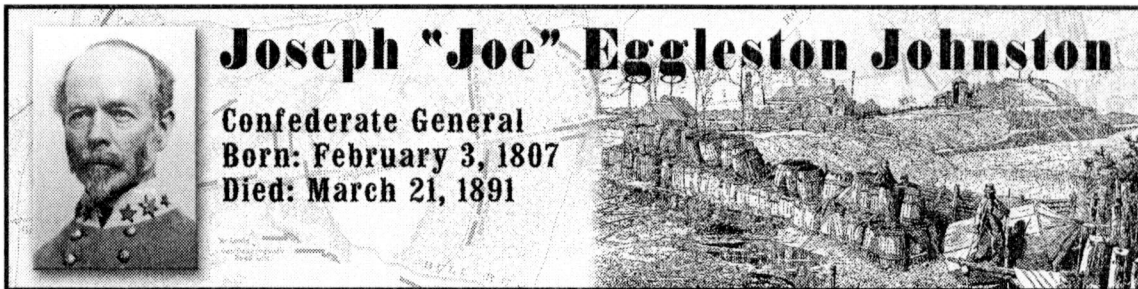

Joseph "Joe" Eggleston Johnston

Confederate General
Born: February 3, 1807
Died: March 21, 1891

When the Civil War began, few soldiers had enjoyed a U.S. Army career as distinguished and honorable as Joseph "Joe" Eggleston Johnston. The Farmville, Virginia, native was the son of an American Revolution veteran. Johnston was a graduate of the West Point class of 1829 and a classmate of Robert E. Lee. Johnston participated in the Black Hawk War, served on the frontier, and fought in the Seminole Wars.

During the Mexican-American War, Johnston was injured five times and received three field promotions. After the war, he served in Texas and Kansas, and he participated in the Utah expedition under Albert Sidney Johnston (the two were not related).

As the Civil War loomed on the horizon in 1860, Johnston was promoted to brigadier general and named quartermaster of the army. When war erupted, Johnston made the difficult decision to leave the U.S. Army. He said, "I must go with the South, though the action is in the last degree ungrateful...Though I am resigning my position, I trust I may never draw my sword against my flag."

NATIONAL PARK SERVICE

Sydney S. King painted Capture of Ricketts' Battery. The painting is on display at the Henry Hill Visitor Center at Manassas National Battlefield Park in Virginia.

Johnston was appointed a brigadier general in the Confederate army and given control of Rebel forces in northern Virginia. Johnston did draw his sword against his former country when Union General Irvin McDowell brought the war to him at Bull Run.

FIRST BULL RUN

In July 1861, many Union soldiers were nearing the end of their three-month enlistment. Lincoln ordered McDowell and his 35,000 men into action. McDowell moved slowly towards Manassas Junction. His inexperienced troops struggled to remove felled trees, stopped often for imagined enemies, and ran out of food.

Johnston heard of McDowell's advance from Rose O'Neal Greenhow, a Confederate spy inside Washington social circles. McDowell's setbacks allowed Johnston to move many of his troops by rail to reinforce P.G.T. Beauregard at Manassas Junction. Johnston was the ranking officer but deferred to Beauregard since he was familiar with the area and defenses. The two men deployed about 30,000 Confederate troops along and near Bull Run Creek and waited for McDowell.

Early in the war, soldiers and civilians on both sides held a romantic view of battle. Many civilians accompanied the Union Army to Manassas Junction. Some even brought picnic baskets in anticipation of watching the battle much

General Irwin McDowell

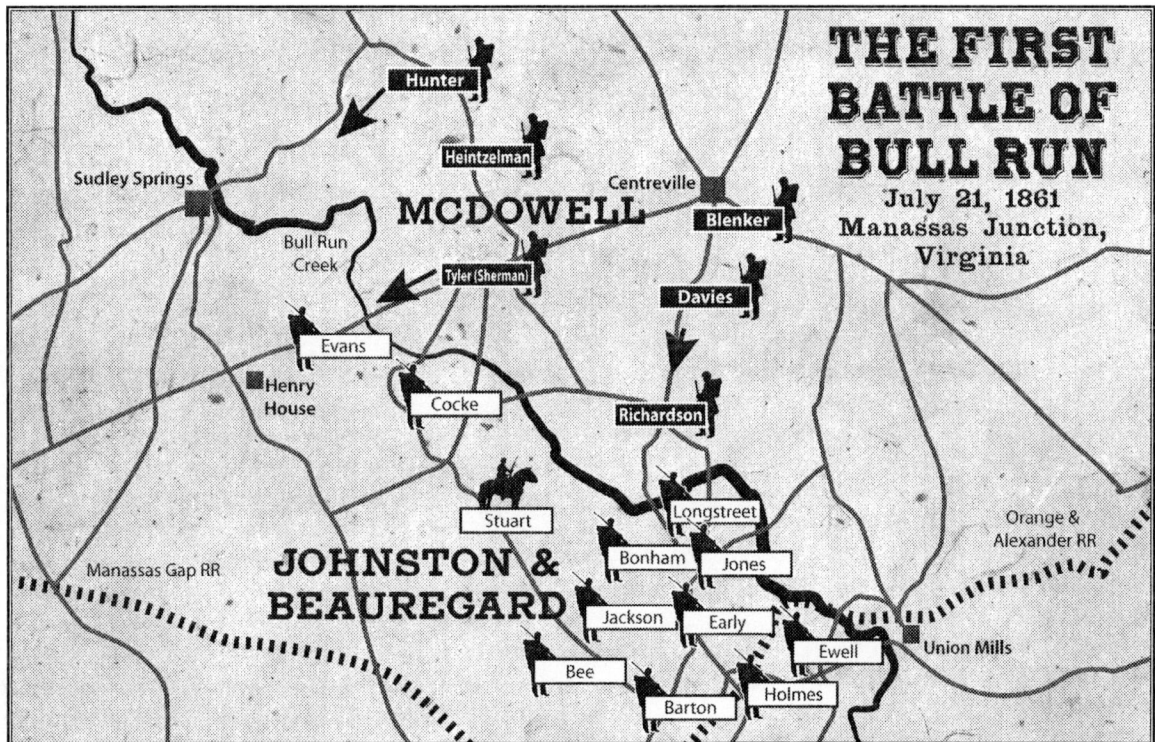

like one would watch a play or sporting event. The gruesome violence of First Battle of Bull Run would shatter any ideals about a short and glorious conflict.

McDowell's plan of attack was sound. His main force would attack the Rebel flank from the north while a secondary force attacked from

THE FIRST BATTLE OF BULL RUN
July 21, 1861
Manassas Junction, Virginia

the front in order to hold the Rebels in place. The flanking force forded Bull Run Creek unnoticed by the Confederates. Once the battle was joined, confusion ensued. Soldiers on both sides had limited training. A variety of uniforms—or lack thereof—contributed to the confusion. No one was prepared for the deadliness of improved cannons and rifled muskets.

McDowell's attack succeeded in turning the flank, slowly pushing back the Rebels. A Union victory appeared imminent. Colonel Thomas Jackson's Virginia brigade held the line near the Henry House Hill until the Confederates could organize a counterattack. Federal officers lost control of their units and soldiers began a panicked retreat back towards Washington, sweeping up the shocked civilians as they went.

Miles from the battlefield, terrified soldiers continued the panicked retreat, refusing to stop even under threat of being shot by officers. The death toll was light compared to many future battles. Union casualties came to about 2,700, with 418 dead; Confederate casualties were about 2,000 with a similar number of dead.

After the battle, newspapers criticized Union leaders for not properly leading their men. Many soldiers complained they did not fight simply because they lacked orders. Confederate leadership had succeeded in stopping the Union attack, but it failed to capitalize on the Union's retreat. In reality, a lack of supplies, heavy rain, and a defensive line of fresh Union troops deployed in defenses guarding Washington, D.C., made a southern advance near impossible. Ultimately, a lack of experience by leaders and troops on both sides prevented either from claiming complete victory when the time and conditions presented it.

An observation by a citizen of Richmond shortly after the First Battle of Bull Run foreshadowed many of the grisly scenes to come:

Little remained of Judith Henry's House after the First Battle of Bull Run.

"The whole city was there...all strained forward in the same intent gaze, as car after car was emptied of its ghastly freight. There, under the pitiless storm, they stood silent and still, careless of its fury—not a sound breaking the perfect hush, in which the measured tramp of the carriers, or the half-repressed groan of the wounded sounded painfully distinct."

QUARREL WITH PRESIDENT DAVIS

A month after Bull Run, President Jefferson Davis promoted five men, including Johnston, to full general. Johnston was offended because Davis had promoted him fifth, when Johnston had outranked all four of the other men when in the U.S. Army. The men ahead of Johnston were Samuel Cooper, A.S. Johnston, Robert E. Lee, and P.G.T. Beauregard.

This incident launched a feud between Davis and Johnston that would last long after

Jefferson Davis

the war. Davis wanted aggressive, offensive-minded generals. Johnston knew the South did not have strong offensive capabilities. He would fight defensively, trading space for time, in an effort to outlast the enemy.

SEVEN PINES

Johnston put his defensive tactics to good use during the Peninsula Campaign. He waited until swollen rivers forced George McClellan to split his army in May 1862. Johnston attacked the weaker Union column in one of the few battles where the Rebels had superiority of numbers.

Misunderstood orders and confusion among lower-ranking officers prevented the Rebel units from coordinating their attacks. Most of the fighting took place in small pockets in thick forests and flooded low areas that negated Johnston's greater numbers.

The attack faltered when General Edwin "Bull" Sumner succeeded in moving his division across waterlogged bridges to reinforce Union positions. During the battle, Johnston was injured severely by shell fragments and bullet in the shoulder. Davis seized the opportunity to replace Johnston with Lee.

THE WESTERN THEATER

After recovering from his wounds, Johnston took command in the Western Theater. Johnston saw the appointment as an attempt to get him out of way, saying that it was a "nominal and useless" command. Johnston's primary concern was dealing with Ulysses S. Grant's campaign to capture Vicksburg. Davis wanted Johnston to rescue Vicksburg's besieged forces under General John Pemberton. Johnston wanted Pemberton to break out of Vicksburg and join his forces. Together, he planned that they would defeat Grant and retake Vicksburg.

D.O.D. MEDIA

The Battle of Seven Pines was one of the first in which observation balloons were used to gather information about enemy forces. This Union balloon was named the *Intrepid*.

John Pemberton

LIBRARY OF CONGRESS

This painting by William McIlvaine illustrates one of the two bridges built over the Chickahominy River by General Edwin "Bull" Sumner's men.

Pemberton's force was too weak to break out of Vicksburg. Grant charged William T. Sherman with guarding the Union's rear. Johnston's five divisions could not match Sherman's seven. After the fall of Vicksburg, a furious Jefferson Davis blamed Johnston. Vicksburg fell, he said, because of "...a general outside who wouldn't fight."

The Atlanta and Carolina Campaigns

The Army of Tennessee was in disarray after the disastrous Chattanooga campaign in November 1863. Johnston assumed command from Braxton Bragg, reorganizing the army and bolstering morale. Johnston was given the unenviable job of slowing Sherman's advance on Atlanta.

A cycle emerged where Johnston would set up defensive positions. Sherman then flanked the positions with his much-larger army. Johnston would withdraw and establish a new line until it too was flanked. The withdrawals frustrated Davis, who removed Johnston shortly before the Battle of Atlanta. Johnston was replaced by John Bell Hood, who proved ineffective in defending Atlanta.

John Bell Hood

Davis reluctantly sent Johnston to the Carolinas in February 1865 to attempt to stop Sherman's march northward. Johnston admired Sherman's resolve to press through the Salk swamps, which he had thought impossible. Johnston said, "I made up my mind that there had been no such army in existence since the days of Julius Caesar."

Johnston combined remnants of Hood's Army of the Tennessee, South Carolinians under Wade Hampton, and other small units to challenge Sherman. Johnston received word that 30,000 Union troops were moving inland from the coast to join Sherman. Johnston made one last attack against Sherman near Bentonville, North Carolina, on March 19th. The initial attack was a success, but the weight of Union reinforcements turned the battle. With Lee having already surrendered, and with nothing left to fight for, Johnston surrendered to Sherman near Durham Station, North Carolina, on April 26, 1865.

The Feud Continues

After the war, Johnston started an insurance agency. The success of his business allowed him time to write his memoirs and continue his feud with Davis. Unlike Davis, Sherman, and Grant spoke highly of Johnston in their postwar writings. Johnston served as a congressman from Virginia from 1879 to 1881.

Johnston served as an honorary pallbearer at the funeral of his former rival, Sherman in February 1891. The day of the funeral was rainy and cold. Out of respect for his former adversary, Johnston removed his hat. As a result, he contracted pneumonia from which he never recovered. Johnston died in Washington, D.C., on March 21, 1891.

Few, if any, men were directly involved in more campaigns of the Civil War than Joseph E. Johnston. Along with Lee, Johnston understood how the South should fight under the circumstances. He made the best of his limited resources. Johnston could not win the war, but without him, the South might easily have exhausted itself much sooner.

Sterling Price

Confederate Politician and General
Born: September 14, 1809
Died: September 29, 1867

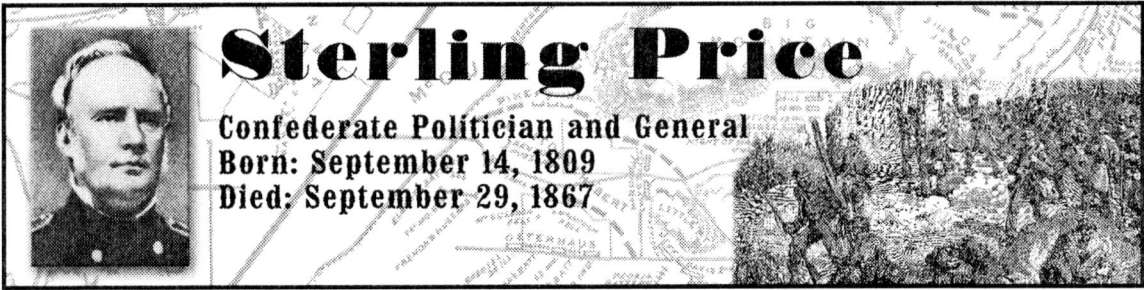

If asked to name important Civil War battles, most people would list battles in the Eastern Theater, such as Gettysburg, Antietam, and Fredericksburg. Though the western battles were typically smaller engagements, they were many. In fact, only two states—Virginia and Tennessee—witnessed more battles and skirmishes than Missouri. One of the Famous Men who fought battles west of the Mississippi River was Missourian Sterling Price.

Price was born in Virginia in 1809 to a middle-class tobacco-farming family of Welsh descent. As a young man, he attended Hampden-Sydney College and appeared destined for a career in law. A turning point occurred in 1830 when his family moved to Keytesville, Missouri.

In Keytesville, Sterling married, fathered seven children, and became an important part of the community. The owner of twelve slaves, he oversaw a prosperous tobacco farm. Sterling was described as a tall, handsome man with dignified features. His neighbors admired his intellect and charm, leading them to elect Price to the state legislature on their own initiative. In 1844, he was elected to represent Missouri in the U.S. House of Representatives.

THE MEXICAN-AMERICAN WAR AND GOVERNORSHIP

When the Mexican-American War broke out, Price resigned in order to lead Missouri volunteers. The regiment of cavalry he raised elected him as its colonel. Price contracted cholera during the trip to Santa Fe, resulting in lifelong problems that ultimately contributed to his death. Though he had no military training, he successfully quelled the Pueblo Indian

uprisings and captured the Mexican city of Chihuahua. He did face criticism for allowing his men to kill 200 Mexican troops, many of whom had surrendered.

Price returned home as a hero and a brigadier general. One of the most popular men in Missouri, he was elected governor in 1853. As a slave owner himself, he supported entry of Kansas as a slave state. He did not lend aid to border ruffians who crossed into Kansas in order to terrorize slavery opponents, but he did not stand in their

Nathaniel Lyon, commander of the U.S. Army garrison in St. Louis

way. When the Civil War began, he was working as a bank commissioner.

Because Missouri was a border state, both Confederate and Union groups could count on strong support. Most of the pro-slave citizens who lived in the middle of the state on large farms favored the Confederacy. St. Louis was the power center for pro-Union sentiment. German immigrants organized by Frank P. Blair Jr. and Nathaniel Lyon, commander of the U.S. Army garrison in St. Louis, ensured that St. Louis supported the Union. Most Missourians fell somewhere in between; they just wished to remain neutral.

In February of 1861, Price led a state convention called to consider secession. To the chagrin of the southern-leaning state government, the delegates, including Price, voted 89 to 1 to remain in the Union.

Shortly after the attack on Fort Sumter, Governor Claiborne Jackson sent 700 men to seize weapons in St. Louis. In what became known as the Camp Jackson Affair, Lyon led out Union troops to capture them. While marching the captives through St. Louis, a riot broke out and troops fired into the crowd, killing 28 people. The incident electrified the state. Governor Jackson was given absolute power to arm Missouri against the Union. He appointed Price as major general in charge of the Missouri State Guard.

In June, Lyon moved with 7000 troops against Jefferson City. The Confederate government fled, and Lyon replaced it with an anti-slavery government. Lyon then moved to Springfield. Price joined with Confederate General Ben McCulloch's troops. The Confederates, outnumbering Lyon two to one, began planning to attack Lyon at Springfield.

Claiborne Jackson

BATTLE OF WILSON'S CREEK

The first major battle in the Western Theater took place near Wilson's Creek in southwest Missouri on August 10, 1861. Union Colonel Franz Sigel convinced Lyon to attack Price and McCulloch before they reached Springfield. Lyon sent Sigel with 1200 troops on a flanking maneuver to attack the Rebels from the rear. Lyon kept a main force of about 4000 troops.

Sigel surprised and pursued the Rebels. The offensive ended quickly when he mistook the 3rd Louisiana Regiment for the Union's 1st Iowa (both wore gray uniforms). Sigel's troops were soon routed and fled the field.

Franz Sigel

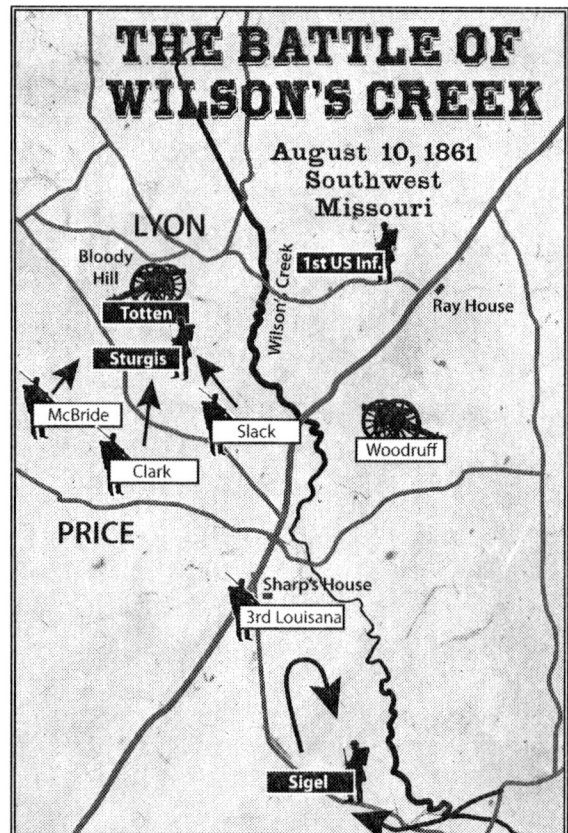

THE BATTLE OF WILSON'S CREEK
August 10, 1861
Southwest Missouri

The John Ray House sits next to the Telegraph Road (marked by rocks) that stretched from Jefferson City, Missouri to Fort Smith, Arkansas. Battles were fought along the road at Wilson's Creek, Pea Ridge, and Prairie Grove. The house was used as a Confederate field hospital during the Battle of Wilson's Creek.

Lyon's troops succeeded in driving the Confederates off of a prominent hill. The Confederate attempt to retake "Bloody Hill" would result in a bitter five-hour battle. Three Confederate attacks failed to seize the hill but wore down the Union soldiers. Lyon suffered two injuries before he was killed while leading a counter charge. Major Samuel Sturgis took command after Lyon's death. Low on ammunition, Sturgis ordered the Federal troops to withdraw. Each side sustained over 1200 casualties.

The battle was a Confederate victory. However, the exhausted Rebels were in no position to pursue the Union forces or take Springfield. Ironically, the battle essentially assured that Missouri would remain under Union control. Lyon was the first Union general to assume the offensive during the war. He was also the first general to die.

An artillery piece sits atop Bloody Hill at Wilson's Creek National Battlefield.

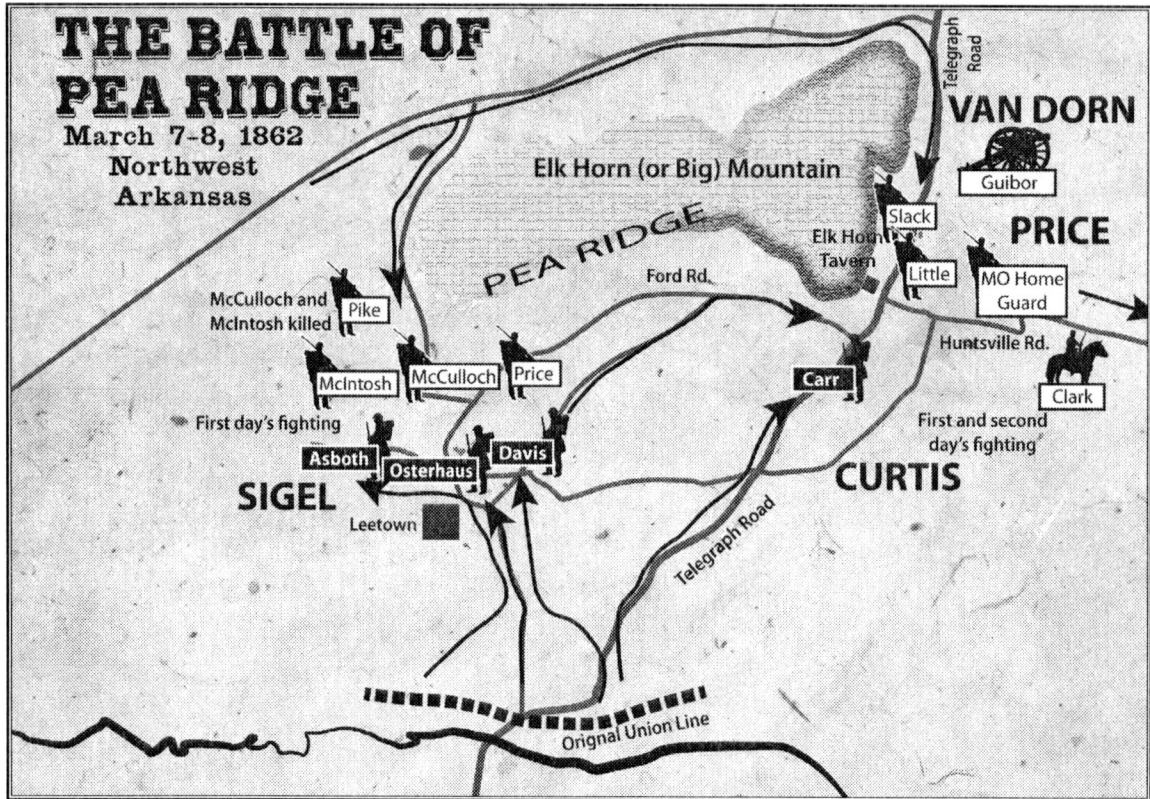

THE BATTLE OF PEA RIDGE
March 7-8, 1862
Northwest Arkansas

VAN DORN

Guibor

PRICE

Elk Horn (or Big) Mountain

Slack

Elk Horn Tavern

Little

MO Home Guard

Ford Rd.

PEA RIDGE

Huntsville Rd.

McCulloch and McIntosh killed

Pike

McIntosh

McCulloch

Price

Carr

Clark

First and second day's fighting

First day's fighting

CURTIS

Asboth

Osterhaus

Davis

SIGEL

Leetown

Telegraph Road

Orignal Union Line

Telegraph Road

BATTLE OF PEA RIDGE

In early 1862 Price's Missouri Home Guard and McCulloch's army were unified under the command of Major General Earl Van Dorn. The 16,000 Rebels gathered near Fayetteville, Arkansas in anticipation of retaking Missouri.

Union troops under General Samuel Curtis dug in near Elkhorn Mountain in northwest Arkansas to stop the Rebel advance. Van Dorn decided to attack from the rear by making a forced march north of Elkhorn Mountain.

McCulloch's troops fell behind and Van Dorn redirected them south of Elkhorn Mountain. Dividing his army and leaving baggage and ammunition behind proved to be critical mistakes. McCulloch's

Earl Van Dorn

troops included two regiments of Cherokee under General James McIntosh. A group of 600 Union troops opened fire on McCulloch's men, but were eventually pushed back. McCulloch and the next two ranking officers were killed while scouting out Union positions. Without leadership, the attack faltered and few of McCulloch's troops managed to rejoin Van Dorn's army.

On the east side of Elkhorn Mountain, Price's Missourians successfully drove back the Union soldiers, capturing Elk Horn Tavern and a critical road junction along Telegraph Road before darkness fell on March 7th, 1862.

Overnight, the entire Union Army formed one continuous line, with Curtis commanding

Samuel Curtis

A replica of Elk Horn Tavern, complete with elk horns on the crest of the roof, is open to visitors at Pea Ridge National Military Park.

two divisions on the right and Franz Sigel commanding two on the left. Curtis preceded a counterattack early the next morning with a 21-cannon artillery barrage. The Confederates resisted stoutly near Elk Horn Tavern, but broke under the weight of Union infantry and a lack of ammunition caused by Van Dorn's foolish decision. By 9:30 a.m., Van Dorn's army dissolved in a disorderly retreat.

The decisive loss led Confederate leaders to conclude that Missouri was a lost cause. Missouri would remain firmly in Union hands for the remainder of the war. The Federals suffered 1384 casualties; the Rebels about 2000.

BATTLE OF PRAIRIE GROVE

After Pea Ridge, Curtis tasked armies under generals James Blunt and Francis J. Herron with clearing northwest Arkansas of Rebels. General Thomas C. Hindman opposed this move with a plan to destroy each army individually with his larger force.

On December 7, 1862, Hindman attacked Herron's cavalry near Prairie Grove, Arkansas. The Confederates formed a line on a wooded ridge near the Borden house. The two sides exchanged assaults with little success. Blunt followed the sound of the fighting and joined Herron late in the day. The results were the same. In spite of the more than 2500 combined casualties Prairie Grove is often described as a "forgotten" battle that settled little.

Thomas C. Hindman

The Prairie Grove Campaign ended several weeks later when Hindman was defeated at the Battle of Van Buren. There was no sizable Confederate army in Arkansas for the remainder of the war.

MISSOURI RAID OF 1864

As Missouri's 1864 elections neared, General Edmund Kirby Smith and exiled Missouri gover-

Rebel soldiers formed a line in front of the Borden House during the Battle of Prairie Grove. Today the house is part of Prairie Grove Battlefield State Park.

nor Thomas Reynolds formulated a plan to bring Missouri back into the Confederacy. They would send Price with 12,000 men on a raid to rally supporters, collect supplies, and install a Confederate government by capturing Jefferson City.

Price's first goal was to capture supplies at St. Louis. Price went against the advice of his officers and chose to attack, rather than bypass, Fort Davidson. Price succeeded in capturing the fort during the Battle of Pilot Knob. However, the battle cost Price casualties which he could not afford and convinced him to change his plans.

Price decided to move directly against Jefferson City. When he heard that the city had been heavily reinforced, he once again changed his plans and headed west towards Kansas City. Price was stopped by his old nemesis, Samuel Curtis, at Westport, Missouri.

The Battle of Westport was the largest engagement in the Western Theater based on total number of soldiers with about 30,000 involved. Price was greatly outnumbered by the 22,000 troops of Curtis' Army of the Border. Confederate forces under Generals James F. Fagan and Joseph O. Shelby pushed back Blunt's Union forces long enough to allow Price to escape across the Blue River. Blunt moved artillery into position and punished the Confederates as they retreated southward. Union forces harassed Price's weary and demoralized troops, eventually driving them into the Indian Territory.

After the war, Price's supporters provided him with a house in St. Louis. His ongoing struggles with cholera led to his death on September 29, 1867. In 1915, the residents of Keytesville erected a monument to Price. No matter where their sympathies may have been, Price had earned widespread respect among Missourians both as a governor and general.

A mural at the Missouri State Capitol depicts the struggle for Brush Creek during the Battle of Westport.

David Glasgow Farragut

Union Naval Admiral
Born: July 5, 1801
Died: August 14, 1870

A Spanish merchant captain, and descendant of a 13th Century Spanish conquistador, Jordi Farragut arrived in the American colonies in 1766. Jordi joined the cause for freedom and fought the British during the American Revolution as part of South Carolina's continental navy. After the war, he married a Scotch-Irish woman named Elizabeth and the couple had a son, James Glasgow Farragut. At age four, young Farragut embarked on his first naval adventure, a 1700-mile flatboat ride from Tennessee to New Orleans.

James' mother died when he was only seven years old. His father sent him to live with a family friend, David Porter, who was a naval veteran of the Barbary Wars. The Porters adopted James, and he changed his first name to "David" in honor of his foster father. Farragut's adoptive brother, David Dixon Porter, would also see extensive naval service during the Civil War.

At age nine, Farragut began service as a midshipman. He first saw combat during the War of 1812 while onboard Porter's ship, the USS *Essex*. Farragut proved unafraid to fight during a two-hour battle that claimed the lives of 58 *Essex* crewmembers. His first command was to bring the captured British ship *Barclay* to port during the war.

After the war, Farragut served in fleets in the Mediterranean and Caribbean His first wife died in 1840. Farragut remarried in 1843 to Virginia Loyall Farragut. She was the mother of his only surviving son, Loyall Farragut.

Farragut commanded the USS *Saratoga* on blockade duty during the Mexican-American War but did not see combat. During the 1850s, he supervised construction of the first U.S. naval base on the Pacific coast—the Mare Island, California naval yards.

When the Civil War began, Farragut had already served in the U.S. Navy for over 50 years. Farragut and his family were living in Virginia when war began. Southerners wanted him to fight for the South. Farragut refused. He said, "Mind what I tell you: You fellows will catch the devil before you get through with this business." Farragut and his family fled to New York.

NATIONAL ARCHIVES

David Farragut wears the uniform of a Rear Admiral in 1863.

BATTLE OF NEW ORLEANS

Farragut's long and distinguished record caught the attention of Secretary of the Navy Gideon Welles. In 1862, Welles named Farragut commander of the West Gulf Blockading Squadron. His command ship was the sloop-of-war USS *Hartford*.

Farragut prepared to take New Orleans from the Rebels. Capturing New Orleans would close an important port to Confederate blockade runners and was an important step in controlling the Mississippi River. Farragut formed a fleet with fourteen gunboats, nineteen mortar schooners, and eight steam sloops that could easily navigate the Mississippi River sand bars.

If the formidable fleet was not enough, the city of New Orleans was already in a precarious position. Most soldiers in Louisiana had been sent north to check General U.S. Grant's march towards Corinth. New Orleans' few defenders manned forts downstream from the city.

On April 18, 1862, Farragut began a bombardment of 3000 shells daily against the forts. It lasted six days. The bombardment did little to reduce the fort's fighting power. Two Union gunboats cleared a path by cutting a chain strung across the river supported by abandoned ships. The forts, several wooden gunboats, and the moored ironclad CSS *Louisiana* attacked the Union fleet as it steamed upriver. Every Union ship that passed through was damaged and suffered casualties; however, the only Union ship sunk was the 10-gun sloop *Varuna*.

Farragut's fleet arrived unopposed at New Orleans on April 25th. Marines raised U.S. flags over the public buildings of the defenseless city despite the protests of citizens. General Benjamin Butler entered the city on May 1st with 5000 soldiers to occupy it for the duration of the war.

The citizens of New Orleans resented the Union occupation. Women cast hateful glances, screamed curses, or crossed the street to avoid Union soldiers. Farragut even had a chamber pot emptied on his head by a wrathful woman shortly after he occupied the city. Butler issued General Order No. 28 stating that any woman who showed

Benjamin Butler

contempt would be treated as if a prostitute. Despite howls of protests across the South, the order had its intended effect in limiting behavior intended to cause an uprising.

Over the next couple of months, Farragut's fleet moved up the river and succeeded in capturing Baton Rouge and Natchez. His attempts to capture Vicksburg failed. The city would not fall until Grant forced its surrender in July 1863.

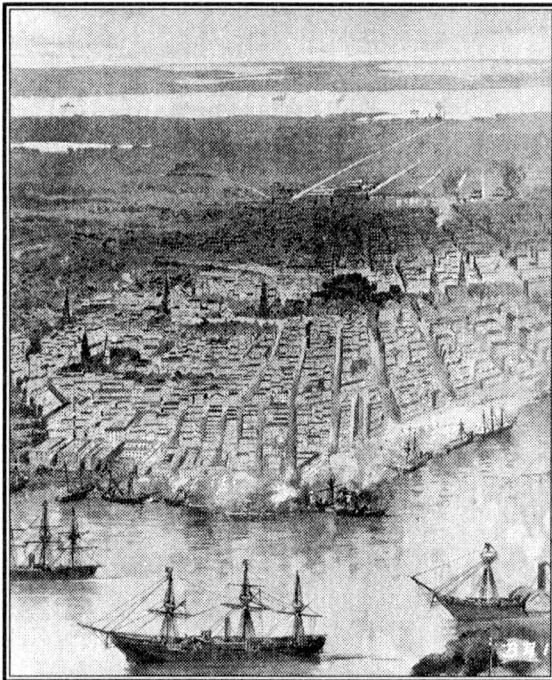

Union naval ships sail in the Mississippi River at New Orleans.

THE PHOTOGRAPHIC HISTORY OF THE CIVIL WAR

Farragut and his officers stand on the deck of the USS *Hartford*.

BATTLE OF MOBILE BAY

By August 1864, the Anaconda Plan had limited the Confederates to two open ports: Galveston, Texas, and Mobile Bay, Alabama. Galveston was of minor concern, so Farragut was tasked with closing Mobile Bay to blockade runners.

The Confederates only had a small fleet under Admiral Franklin Buchanan consisting of the sidewheel wooden gunboats *Selma*, *Morgan*, and *Gaines* and a single ironclad, the CSS *Tennessee*. The strength of the southern defense was three forts guarding the entrance to Mobile Bay with a total of 104 large guns and a field of submerged torpedoes. At the time, immobile naval mines were called torpedoes.

The Union battle plan was to launch a coordinated land and naval attack. On August 3rd, General Gordon Granger landed 5500 troops on Dauphin Island to attack Fort Gaines. Two days later, Farragut led 14 wooden ships, including his flagship *Hartford*, and four ironclads into the bay with the intent to push quickly past the forts.

Farragut climbed the rigging to get a better view of signals from the leading ships. A crew member tied him to the mast so he could not fall off if he or the ship was struck.

The ships passed near Fort Morgan in two parallel columns. The ironclads formed one column on the side facing the fort in order to protect the wooden ships. The ironclad *Tecumseh* led the way, followed by *Brooklyn* and the *Hartford*. The *Tecumseh* survived fire from Fort Gaines and the *Tennessee* before striking a mine, capsizing, and sinking in less than 30 seconds. The *Tecumseh's* Commander, Tunis A. M. Craven, and 89 of his 114 men perished.

Horrified by what happened to the *Tecumseh*, Captain James Alden Jr. of the *Brooklyn* gave the order to pull back. Farragut knew stopping was not an option as the collapsing columns of ships would create easy targets for the forts. The exact wording of his next order is debated, but it has been paraphrased as, "Damn the torpedoes, full speed ahead." Farragut's resolve to press forward

James Alden, Jr.

secured his place in naval military history. The slow *Tennessee* could only offer token resistance as the *Hartford* successfully navigated the minefield. As the other ships followed, several hit waterlogged torpedoes that failed to explode.

Buchanan retreated, allowed his men to eat breakfast, and then began to pursue the Union fleet. Farragut saw the *Tennessee* approaching and turned his ship to meet her. The two ships engaged in a slow-motion game of chicken. At the last second, the two ships swerved to slip past one another. Sailors on both ships hurled insults and any objects that they could find. A sailor on the *Tennessee* even stabbed one on the *Hartford*. Soon, Union ships surrounded the *Tennessee* and pummeled her.

THE BATTLE OF MOBILE BAY

August 5, 1864
Southern
Alabama

Mississippi River

Mobile

MOBILE BAY

Buchanan's Fleet

Fort Powell

Fort Morgan

Dauphin Island

Fort Gaines

Farragut's Fleet

GULF OF MEXICO

The Battle of Mobile Bay was one of the most significant naval battles of the war. It had taken more than three years, but Winfield Scott's Anaconda Plan had wrapped its final coil around the South. After the battle, Congress awarded Farragut a $50,000 bonus that would be worth millions today. Farragut was promoted to Vice Admiral in December 1864.

A WELL-DESERVED PROMOTION

On July 26, 1866, Farragut was promoted to full admiral. It was a new position created by Congress specifically for him. The next year, he made a goodwill tour of Europe onboard his flagship *Franklin*.

Achieving glory as a war hero was not enough to make Farragut seek retirement. He stayed on active duty until his death in 1870. While visiting Portsmouth, New Hampshire, he suffered a fatal heart attack. His family buried his remains in Woodlawn Cemetery in the Bronx. Five U.S. Navy ships have been named for Farragut. The most recent, the Arleigh Burke-class destroyer USS *Farragut* (DDG-99) was commissioned in 2006.

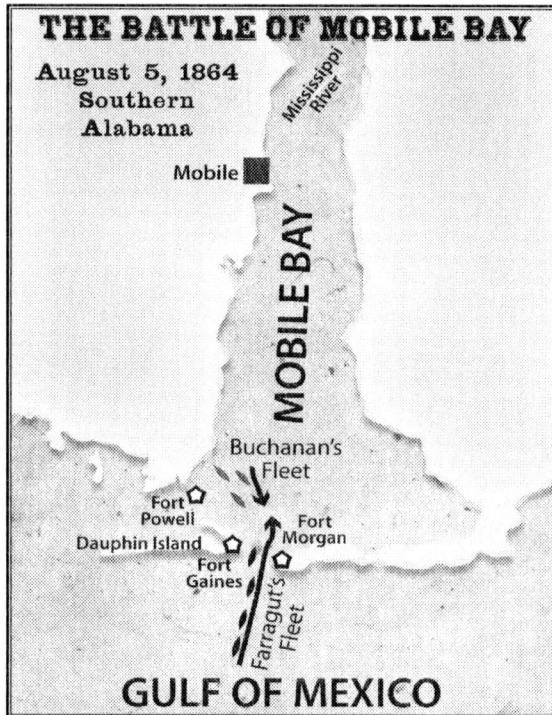

Buchanan surrendered, but not until after he was seriously injured by an exploding shell.

The Union left the well-defended city of Mobile alone, but it had succeeded in closing the bay to Confederate blockade runners.

This Julian O. Davidson painting shows the Union column passing by Fort Morgan.

George Brinton McClellan

Union General & Politician
Born: December 3, 1826
Died: October 29, 1885

The most prominent Union military leader in the early part of the war was George Brinton "Mac" McClellan. McClellan was born to a prominent Philadelphia family in 1826. The great-grandson of Revolutionary War General Samuel McClellan, he entered West Point at the age of 15. There, he befriended southern cadets whom he would later fight against, including Ambrose P. Hill. He graduated second in his class ahead of Jonathan "Stonewall" Jackson and George Pickett in 1846.

During the Mexican War, Mac displayed road building skills and bravery that earned him rapid promotion. After the wa,r he taught at West Point and observed the Crimean War in central Europe in 1856. His observation of Hungarian cavalry saddles led to adoption of the "McClellan saddle" used by the U.S. Army until World War II. In 1857, he resigned from the military and became the chief engineer of Illinois Central Railroad.

McClellan was president of Ohio & Mississippi Railroad when the war began. Because of his military experience, he was appointed General of Ohio volunteers. His organizational abilities gained the attention of President Abraham Lincoln who needed leaders to build an army.

THE RELUCTANT GENERAL

One of McClellan's first assignments was leading the Army of the Ohio to secure West Virginia for the Union. Despite victory, Mac showed a timidity in pursuing the Confederates that would characterize his wartime leadership.

After the Union disaster at First Bull Run, Mac was given charge of the Army of the Potomac. He trained the army and called for the removal of General Winfield Scott. Hailed as "Young Napoleon," Mac replaced Scott as General-in-chief

in November 1861. Lincoln expected McClellan to make a bold move against Richmond. Instead, he hesitated, even refusing once to meet with Lincoln. He refused to share his plans with the President while demanding more troops and supplies.

THE PENINSULA CAMPAIGN

A direct attack from Washington, D.C., towards Richmond would cover 100 miles and require crossing five major rivers. It would also

George McClellan poses with his wife, Mary Ellen.

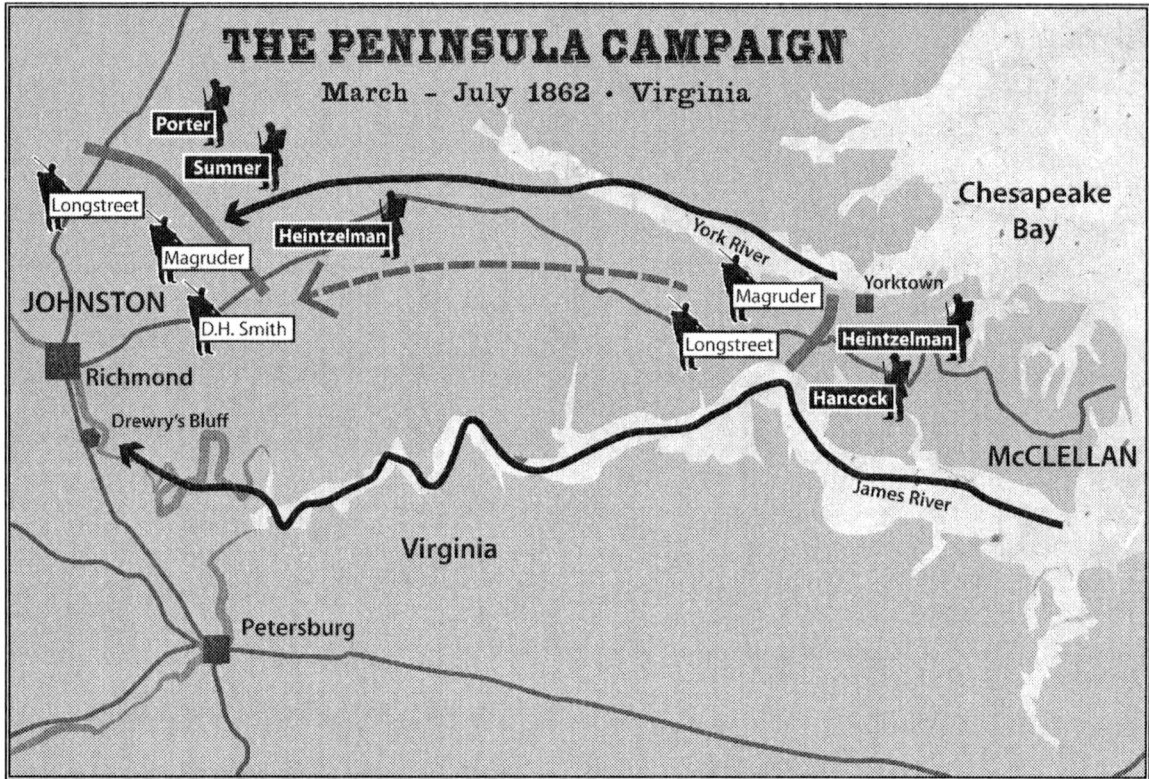

THE PENINSULA CAMPAIGN
March – July 1862 · Virginia

involve attacking Joseph E. Johnston's lines at Manassas Junction. Mac decided to land at the tip of the peninsula formed by the York and James rivers instead. This plan would require crossing two rivers over a 70-mile stretch. Lincoln did not like the plan but gave approval after McClellan agreed to leave enough troops to defend Washington, D.C.

The Union flexed its logistical superiority by using 400 ships and barges to move 100,000 men, hundreds of cannons, and tons of food and equipment into position in March 1862.

Confederate General John B. Magruder's small force entrenched at Yorktown blocked the advance of the Union army. Outnumbered 55,000 to 13,000, Magruder convinced McClellan that he had many more men by parading them around and making noise moving cannons. Lincoln was unhappy when McClellan decided to take Yorktown by siege rather than a direct attack. Lincoln's pleading note on April 9, 1862 finished with "...you must act." Unmoved, McClellan wrote to his wife about Lincoln that "...he had better come do it himself."

While Mac spent weeks at Yorktown, Joe Johnston's army shifted from Manassas Junction to reinforce Magruder. As McClellan slowly maneuvered into position to bombard the Yorktown line, Johnston realized resistance would be pointless. He ordered the retreat of Confederate troops to defensive lines near Richmond. McClellan's approach to Richmond combined with U.S. Grant's victories at Fort Henry and Donelson in the west left many Southerners fearing imminent defeat.

John B.
Magruder

LIBRARY OF CONGRESS

Union soldiers man 13-inch mortars during the siege of Yorktown that was part of the Peninsula Campaign.

Confederate President Jefferson Davis pressured Johnston to act. Johnston attacked elements of the Union Army separated by the swollen Chickahominy River east of Richmond in what became the Battle of Seven Pines. The battle was characterized by many smaller struggles in thick woods and flooded lowlands. The two armies combined for over 11,000 casualties, but the battle settled nothing. The historical significance is that an injury sustained by Johnston during the battle led to his replacement by Robert E. Lee.

The Peninsula Campaign culminated with a series of smaller battles collectively called the Seven Days Battles. Lee built defensive lines to protect Richmond with fewer soldiers, freeing others for an offensive. McClellan continued to delay even after being reinforced by Irvin McDowell's troops. He blamed muddy roads, difficulty in moving artillery into position, and the need to reorganize after Seven Pines. The arrival of Stonewall Jackson's troops fueled Mac's imagination to the point that he believed the rebels had 200,000 troops when they actually had less than 90,000.

The Union attacked first on the June 25th at the Battle of Oak Grove. Union soldiers gained just 600 yards at a cost of over 1000 casual-

ties. Lee's attack the next day also proved futile. Jackson's troops, exhausted from the recent Shenandoah Valley campaign, failed to attack as planned while A.P. Hill's division was mauled by entrenched Union at Mechanicsburg.

The Battle of Gaines' Mill was a southern victory, but once again problems with coordinating attacks proved costly as the South suffered many casualties. Mac felt so threatened by Lee's assault that he abandoned his plan to set up a siege operation around Richmond.

A. P. Hill

Over the next few days, Lee continued to pressure the Union forces with varying success at Savage's Station, Glendale, and White Oak Swamp. The Seven Days Battle culminated with a failed Confederate assault against Malvern Hill on July 1st. Rebel artillery was unable to dislodge Union artillery. Over 5500 southern soldiers were wounded or killed attacking the elevated positions.

Having lost about 25% of his army, Lee decided against further attacks. However, McClellan was completely unnerved and believed all was lost. Against the wishes of his subordinate generals, he continued to retreat.

The Army of the Potomac (AotP) evacuated the peninsula from a secure spot along the James

NATIONAL PARK SERVICE

Robert Sneden painted this view of the battlefield at Malvern Hill.

George McClellan meets with President Abraham Lincoln after the Battle of Antietam.

A campaign poster for the 1864 Presidential election shows Democratic candidate George B. McClellan and his running mate George H. Pendleton.

River. Though appalled by the great losses, driving Union forces away from Richmond boosted southern morale. In contrast, northern morale plummeted. Failure of the campaign that promised to bring the war to a quick end would result in three more years of war.

THE MARYLAND CAMPAIGN

While McClellan retreated and reorganized his army, Lee took the offensive in north Virginia. After defeating General John Pope at Second Bull Run, Lee invaded Maryland in September 1862. With Pope's demoralized forces having retreated into Washington, D.C.'s defenses, only McClellan stood between Lee and the nation's capital.

When a copy of Lee's plan's fell into Union hands, Mac hesitated to use the information to his advantage. Once again, he relied on faulty intelligence suggesting that the rebel army was much larger. Due to McClellan's dawdling, Lee gained time to gather his scattered forces and form a strong defensive line along Antietam Creek.

Despite having almost twice as many troops, uncoordinated Union attacks at Antietam resulted in intense back-and-forth fighting that claimed the lives of over 3600 men and left 17,000 injured. Mac held back one-third of his troops, fearing that they would be crushed by Lee's phantom reserves.

When Lee decided to retreat back to Virginia, McClellan failed to pursue and destroy the rebel army. General-in-chief Henry Halleck summed up the thoughts of Lincoln when he said, "The long inactivity of so large an army in the face of a defeated foe...was a matter of great disappointment and regret."

A DIFFERENT CAMPAIGN

Lincoln had had enough. He removed McClellan from command on November 5, 1862. Mac had a different perspective, as he explained to his wife, "I feel I have done all that can be asked in twice saving the country. ... Well, one of these days history will I trust do me justice."

McClellan spent the next months writing about his campaigns and answering critics. While still on active duty, he entered the 1864 presidential campaign as the Democratic candidate against Lincoln. Many Democrats wanted to cease fighting while McClellan wanted to continue the war but not end slavery. A string of Union victories bolstered Lincoln's vulnerable position shortly before the election. Mac only won three states, losing the Electoral College to Lincoln 212 to 21.

TRAVELS AND GOVERNORSHIP

After the war, Mac traveled with his family in Europe for several years. Upon his return, Mac worked on engineering projects and as president of the Atlantic and Great Western Railroad. Nominated without his knowledge, Mac won election as Governor of New Jersey and served from 1878 to 1881.

In his final years, McClellan traveled and wrote his memoirs, published posthumously and titled *McClellan's Own Story*. Mac died of a heart attack at age 58 in 1887. His final words were, "I feel easy now. Thank you." He was buried in a cemetery in New Jersey.

George McClellan in 1880

George McClellan remains one of the most mystifying figures of the Civil War. His organization of the AotP, the largest Union army and the one that eventually forced the surrender of Lee, is to be praised. He was thought highly of by those under his command. Unfortunately, he failed in almost every way when it came to leading an army into battle. McClellan did not lack personal courage, but he lacked the resolve to command an army.

Albert Sidney Johnston

Confederate General
Born: February 2, 1803
Died: April 6, 1862

The Civil War propelled some men from obscurity to national prominence. Albert Sidney Johnston's story is different. When the war began, the handsome and charming general was one of the most well-known and highly respected officers in the U.S. Army. Due to his untimely death early in the war, few Americans recognize his name today. However, Johnston had a vital impact on one of the greatest—and bloodiest—battles in U.S. history, the Battle of Shiloh.

Johnston was born in 1803 in Washington, Kentucky. He was the youngest son of a country doctor. Albert attended Transylvania University

Albert Sidney Johnston in his Confederate uniform.

along with future Confederate President Jefferson Davis. The two men's friendship continued to grow while they were together at West Point in the mid-1820s.

The Black Hawk War in Illinois and Wisconsin was Johnston's first experience in combat. In 1834, he resigned to care for his ill wife Henrietta. After Henrietta died, Albert joined the Texas army and served during the Texas War for Independence. He quickly rose to Senior Brigadier General.

Johnston was injured during a duel with Texas General Felix Huston. The duel came about after Sam Houston promoted Johnston ahead of Huston and Huston took offense. During the duel, the two men fired three times at each other. Huston hit Johnston in the hip, severing his sciatic nerve. Huston was unharmed. Doctors were certain that Johnston would die, but he recovered after several difficult months

Albert served as the first Secretary of War in the Republic of Texas and led Texas militia as a colonel during the Mexican-American War. He served for a time in the 2nd U.S. Cavalry along with Lieutenant Colonel Robert E. Lee. Johnston's growing resume included leading the Mormon Expedition of 1857 that ensured that the Utah territory remained part of the Union.

When the war began, Johnston was serving as Commander of the Pacific Department in California. His record earned him an offer as second-in-command in the Union Army. Instead, Johnston resigned in order to fight for the South. His old friend Jefferson Davis offered him command of the Western Department, including all Confederate territory west of the Atlantic states.

Shiloh National Military Park has five mass graves for Confederate soldiers. The "Stars and Bars" Confederate flag flies over the grave.

SHILOH

Johnston's assignment was challenging. His determined, but poorly armed and clothed, soldiers were outnumbered two-to-one. After subordinates bumbled into surrendering Fort Henry and Fort Donelson to Ulysses S. Grant, Johnston consolidated 45,000 of his forces to protect the strategic railroad junction at Corinth, Mississippi.

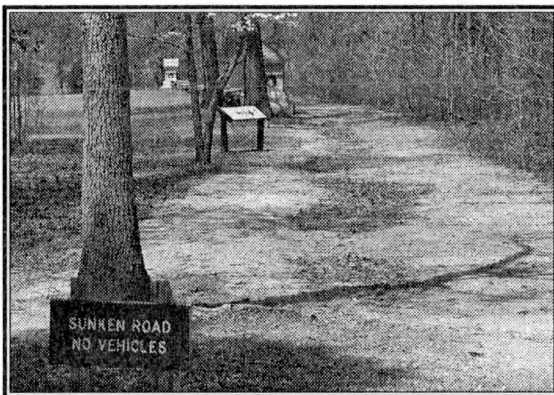

Union General Henry "Old Brains" Halleck gave an order in March 1862 to strike deep into the South via the Tennessee River. Grant took command of the Army of the Tennessee camped near Pittsburg Landing along the river in southern Tennessee. His orders were to wait for General Don Carlos Buell and the Army of the Ohio to arrive, and together they would advance against Corinth. Grant believed Johnston did not have the resolve to make an attack and therefore did not have his men build fortifications.

Henry Halleck

This path marks the location of the Sunken Road at Shiloh National Military Park.

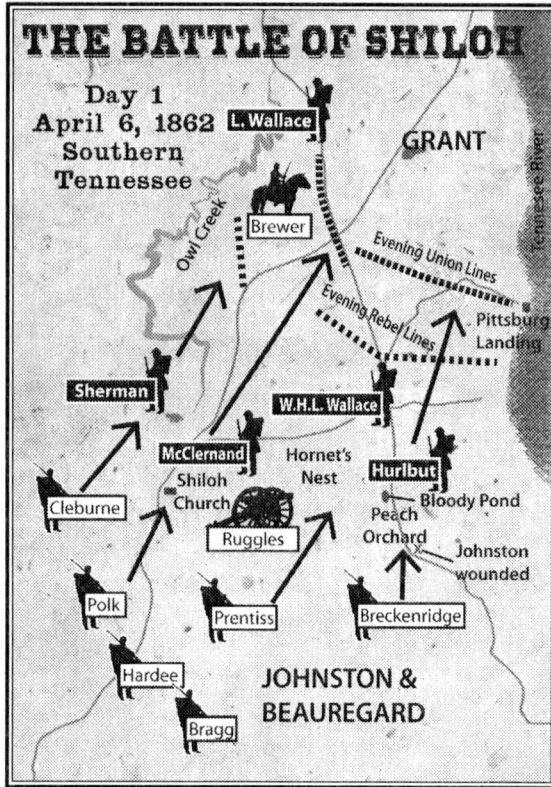

THE BATTLE OF SHILOH

Day 1
April 6, 1862
Southern
Tennessee

GRANT

L. Wallace

Owl Creek

Brewer

Evening Union Lines

Evening Rebel Lines

Pittsburg Landing

Tennessee River

Sherman

W.H.L. Wallace

McClernand

Hornet's Nest

Hurlbut

Shiloh Church

Bloody Pond

Cleburne

Peach Orchard

Ruggles

Johnston wounded

Polk

Prentiss

Breckenridge

Hardee

JOHNSTON & BEAUREGARD

Bragg

Johnston and P.G.T. Beauregard decided to attack Grant before Buell could join him. Beauregard formed a plan by which 38,000 troops would converge at Mickey's farmhouse, eight miles southwest of Pittsburg Landing. The army would then attempt to turn the Union left flank, cutting it off from Pittsburg Landing and trapping it against the swollen Owl Creek.

Johnston hoped to make a one-day march and attack on April 5, 1862. Rain turned the already soft ground into muck, causing delays. The Rebels finally moved into position before dawn on April 6th. At about 5:30 a.m., Johnston mounted his horse, Fire-eater, and told his officers, "Tonight we will water our horses in the Tennessee River."

Union pickets and officers grew increasingly nervous as noise and activity increased in the nearby woods. Nothing prepared them for what happened next. Thousands of screaming rebels attacked divisions under William T. Sherman and Benjamin M. Prentiss. Sherman rode for-

The Shiloh church was destroyed during the battle. This is a replica at Shiloh National Military Park.

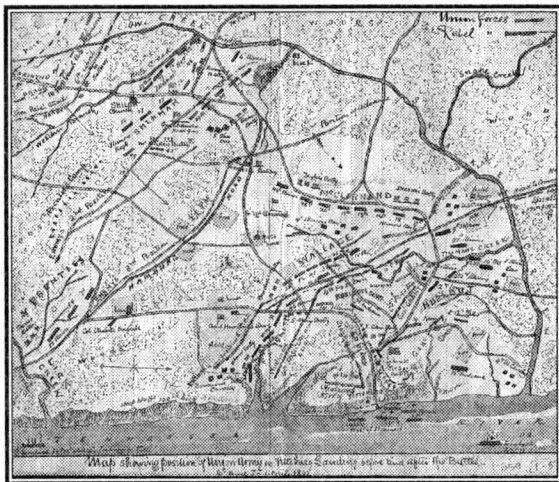

This 1865 map shows the Battle of Shiloh. The top of the map points west.

ward to see what was happening. His orderly was shot and killed, and Sherman was wounded in the hand. He exclaimed, "My God, we are attacked!" and he returned to Shiloh Church to coordinate the defense.

Grant was enjoying breakfast nine miles downriver when he heard the fighting. When he arrived at Pittsburg Landing at 9 a.m., five of his divisions were fiercely engaged with six Confederate divisions. Lew Wallace's division was missing and did not participate in the day's fighting because it had taken the wrong road.

The scene at Pittsburg Landing was one of great confusion. Many of the inexperienced Union soldiers had fled from the front and cowered behind the banks of the Tennessee River. Grant set about reorganizing the troops and artillery into a final line of defense.

Don Carlos Buell

Grant ordered Prentiss to hold a line along a sunken farm road bordering the edge of a field through fierce fighting. Though greatly outnumbered, Prentiss held the Hornet's Nest until late afternoon. As other Union lines fell back, Confederate infantry surrounded the Hornet's Nest and pounded it with over 60 field guns. Prentiss and his 2200 surviving soldiers surrendered at 5:30 p.m.

Johnston personally led an attack against what he believed to be the Union left flank. Instead, he hit the center. The plan to cut off the Union from Pittsburg Landing was faltering. At about 2:30 p.m., while fighting near a Sarah Bell's peach orchard, Johnston was hit by a bullet behind his right knee. The wound would probably have not been serious if Johnston had received immediate medical attention. Instead, Johnston ignored the wound. The continuous loss of blood resulted in Johnston's death within an hour. Beauregard took command of the Rebel army.

Benjamin Prentiss

As twilight descended over the battlefield, Beauregard called off the offensive. After many hours of fighting and the lengthy delay at the Hornet's Nest, he sensed that it was time to reorganize his weary soldiers. The final push would come the next morning. Confident, he sent word to Davis claiming "complete victory." Overnight, few soldiers were able to sleep as a cold, heavy

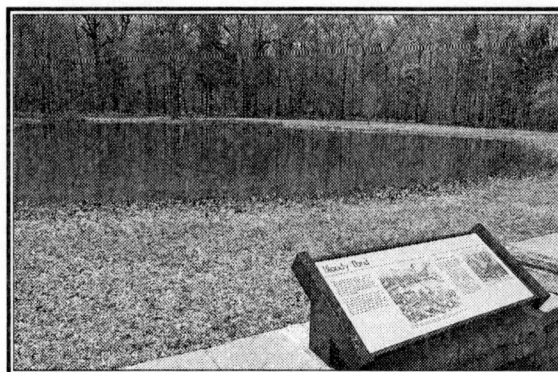

AUTHOR PHOTO

Scholars debate whether or not "Bloody Pond" was actually stained with blood.

SHILOH NATIONAL MILITARY PARK

Union ships dock at Pittsburg Landing several days after the Battle of Shiloh.

rain fell. Some wounded died in brush fires ignited by artillery, while others suffered alone in the rain-soaked mud. Wounded soldiers from both sides dragged themselves to "Bloody Pond" near the peach orchard to get a drink.

The Union Army's situation improved overnight. Elements of Buell's army arrived continuously throughout the night. In addition, Lew Wallace's division finally arrived after having lost its way. Grant had over 20,000 fresh troops to deploy against the Confederates.

Grant spent the night on the field with his soldiers. Some of Grant's officers were convinced that retreat was still the best option. Grant showed his determination by saying, "Retreat? No. I propose to attack at daylight and whip them."

Beauregard spent the night in Sherman's tent near Shiloh church. As dawn broke, the Rebels were met with a surprise attack by Grant and Buell's soldiers. Southern resistance stiffened, but the weight of the Union advance continued to press the Rebels. The fierce fighting retraced the ground covered the previous day as soldiers fought over dead bodies and the lingering wounded. By mid-afternoon, the rebels were pushed back to their original starting point. Beauregard realized his troops' morale was shattered and that retreat was the best option. He gave the order to return to Corinth. Exhausted Union troops set about reorganizing their camps rather than pursuing.

The next day, Sherman pursued Beauregard's army with two brigades. A brief skirmish with Nathan Bedford Forrest's cavalry convinced Sherman that it was best to let the Rebels go.

Shiloh was technically a Union victory. However, northern newspapers criticized Grant for not anticipating the attack and for not pursuing the Confederates afterwards. In fairness, Grant should be credited with preventing total defeat on the first day and seizing the initiative on the second day.

If First Bull Run had established the fact that the war would not be settled by a few battles, Shiloh revealed that the war would be bloodier than anyone could imagine. One Iowa soldier wrote, "For miles the ground was strewn with the mangled remains of the dead and the dying…" Northerners and Southerners alike were shocked to learn that over 23,000 men were casualties of the two-day battle. Bloodier battles would be fought before the war ended, but the casualty toll of this single battle was more than all previous American wars and battles.

Johnston was the highest-ranking official on either side to be killed in combat during the war. The loss of Johnston at Shiloh grieved Jefferson Davis so much that he often said Johnston's death was the turning point in the war. Davis called him "the greatest soldier, the ablest man, civil or military, Confederate or Federal." How differently the war might have progressed if Johnston had lived is a question left to conjecture. Today, Johnston's body rests in the Texas State Cemetery in Austin, Texas.

TRIVIA

Lew Wallace wrote *Ben Hur: A Tale of the Christ*. One of the 19th century's best sellers, the book was adapted into the epic movie *Ben-Hur* in 1959.

Ulysses Simpson Grant

Union General
Born: April 27, 1822
Died: July 23, 1885

The Civil War was a catalyst of great upheaval, raising some men from obscurity to historical immortality while relegating others to the dustbin of history. When the Civil War began, Ulysses Simpson Grant was working as an employee at his father's store in Galena, Illinois. By the end of the war, Grant was the Union's greatest war hero and the architect of victory.

Born Hiram Ulysses Grant in 1822 in Pleasant Point, Ohio, the future war hero described his childhood as uneventful. At age 17, he entered West Point, where he gained a reputation as an excellent horseman.

Grant served as a quartermaster during the Mexican-American War. He participated in the battles of Monterrey, Palo Alto and Veracruz. During the Battle of Chapultepec, Grant helped hoist a howitzer into a church belfry to help clear way for an advance.

Grant served in California before resigning in 1854 to avoid a court-martial. The unconfirmed rumor was that he was a drunk; accusations of drinking would follow Grant throughout his life. Grant was reduced to a meager existence, farming near and selling firewood in St. Louis, Missouri.

As a military leader, Grant was a plain and calm man with a reputation for caring for soldiers. Unlike many Union generals, Grant was aggressive, always fighting and never giving the enemy rest.

After the war began, Grant attended a recruitment meeting in Galena. Being one of the few attendees with military experience, Grant was tasked with recruiting and training volunteers. With the help of Illinois Congressman Elihu B. Washburne, Grant was promoted to colonel, and then brigadier general.

FORTS HENRY AND DONELSON

Grant's first real test was to capture Fort Henry at the mouth of the Tennessee River. On February 6, 1862, seven Union river gunboats attacked the fort. At the same time, 15,000 troops worked their way through swampy terrain towards it. Confederate General Lloyd Tilghman abandoned the fort, sending his troops 11 miles overland to Fort Donelson. The fort guarded the mouth of the Cumberland River.

The next week, the Rebels repulsed a Union gunboat attack against Fort Donelson. As Union troops closed in on the fort, a counterattack by General Gideon Pillow opened the way for the Confederates to escape. Amazingly, Pillow's troops returned to their original lines. The three commanders of the fort—John B. Floyd, Simon B. Buckner, and Pillow—decided to surrender. It

AUTHOR PHOTO

White Haven, near St. Louis, was U.S. Grant's home from 1854 to 1859. Today it is part of the Ulysses S. Grant National Historic Site.

Union troops approach Fort Donelson

was a curious decision. The two forces were al-most equal and the Confederates were in a supe-rior defensive position. Floyd and Pillow slipped away by water, leaving Buckner to surrender the fort and 15,000 men. The loss of Fort Do-nelson is considered the first major Confederate defeat of the war. The victory earned Grant the nickname of "Unconditional Surrender" for the strict terms given to Buckner.

TRIVIA
Confederate General Simon Buckner's son, Simon Buckner, Jr., was the highest ranking American killed during World War II.

SHILOH

Grant's confidence was high after success at Forts Henry and Donelson. He concentrated troops at Pittsburg Landing near Shiloh Church on the Tennessee River from which he antici-pated making a move on Corinth, Mississippi, an important railroad hub.

When the Rebels struck first at Shiloh, Grant tirelessly rallied retreating troops and formed new lines. Instead of retreating overnight as the Confederate officers expected, Grant organized an offensive the next morning that drove the Rebels from the field. Despite saving his army, Grant was accused unfairly afterwards of being completely surprised.

A portion of Grant's canal is still visible today. Depending on the weather, it may be dry or filled with water.

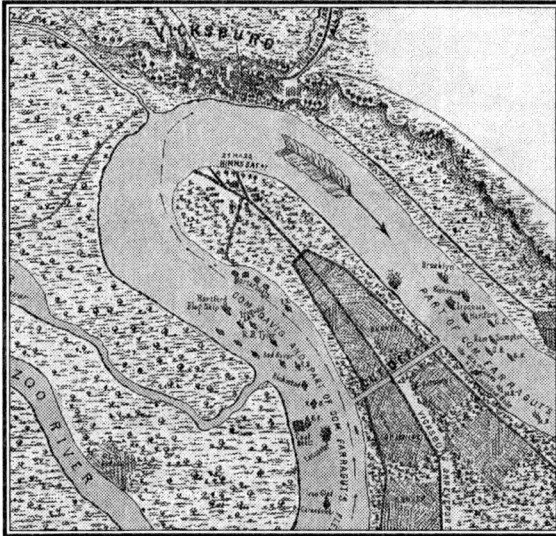

This illustration shows the location of the canal that Grant built across De Soto Point.

THE VICKSBURG CAMPAIGN

Vicksburg, Mississippi, was a vibrant trading and cultural center located on a bend of the Mississippi River. Despite controlling all of the river north and south of the city, the Mississippi's value was greatly diminished because of the bottleneck at Vicksburg. Confederate President Jefferson Davis ordered General John Pemberton to hold the city at all costs. Pemberton turned the city into a fortress with a 6.5-mile defensive line containing 172 artillery positions and strong points. Cannons placed on bluffs over the Mississippi prevented Union steamships from passing.

Capturing Vicksburg proved problematic. Located deep in enemy territory, and surrounded by swampy and rough terrain, the most pressing

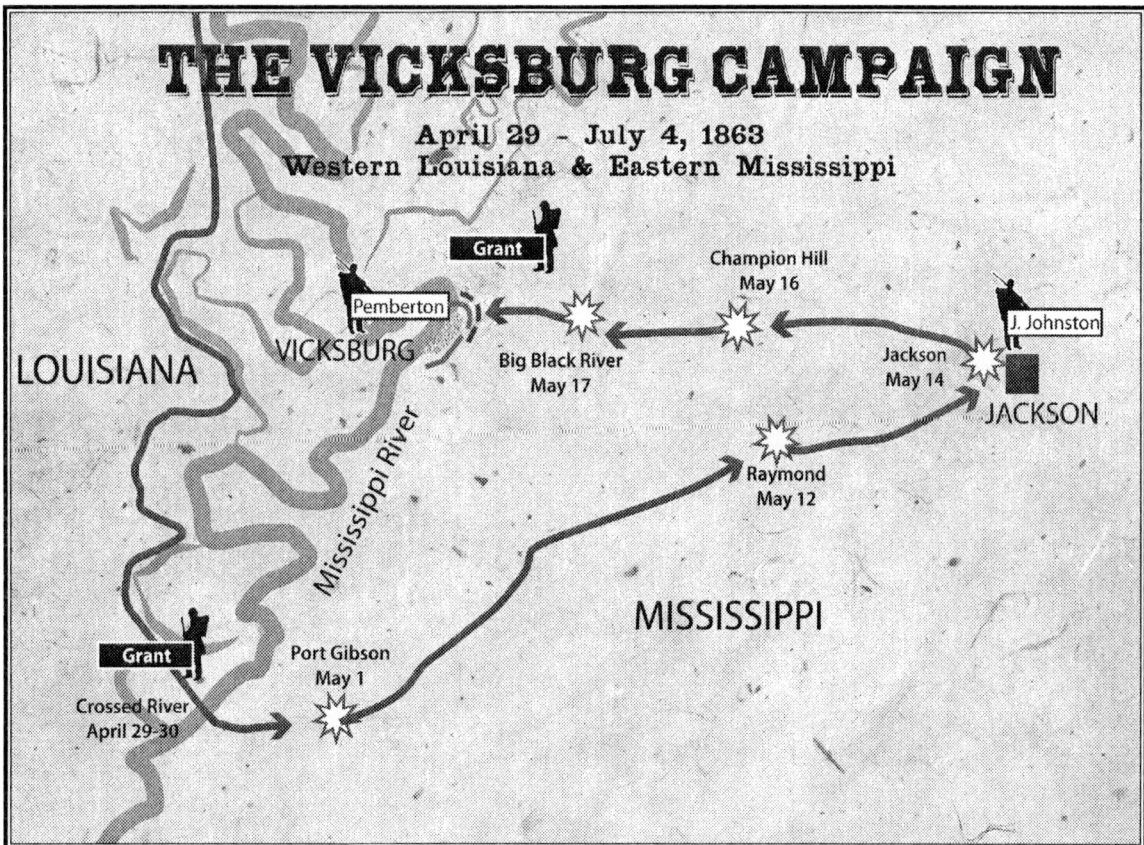

THE VICKSBURG CAMPAIGN
April 29 - July 4, 1863
Western Louisiana & Eastern Mississippi

Grant

Champion Hill
May 16

J. Johnston

Pemberton

VICKSBURG

Big Black River
May 17

Jackson
May 14

JACKSON

LOUISIANA

Mississippi River

Raymond
May 12

MISSISSIPPI

Grant

Port Gibson
May 1

Crossed River
April 29-30

question was simply how to get there. Despite experiencing a number of setbacks, Grant always pressed forward. Perseverance was a quality that endeared him to President Abraham Lincoln. In response to Grant's critic, Lincoln said, "I can't spare this man, he fights."

Admiral David Farragut had failed in several attempts to take Vicksburg from the river. Dissuaded by the near-disaster at Shiloh, Grant decided against an overland march to Vicksburg. His first attempt was to bypass Vicksburg by building a canal across a narrow peninsula in an effort to change the course of the river. Though he thought the effort unlikely to work, he felt it best to keep his men employed.

On December 28, 1862, Grant ordered William T. Sherman to attack at Chickasaw Bluffs north of Vicksburg. The assault failed miserably.

Another grand effort to reach Vicksburg was signaled by a great explosion on February 2, 1863. Union engineers destroyed a levee, opening the Yazoo Pass. A Union squadron sailed down the pass, hoping to reach Vicksburg from the north. The expedition was checked at the improvised Fort Pemberton.

In April, Grant and Admiral David Porter ordered the Mississippi River Squadron to make a risky dash past the Vicksburg batteries. On the night of April 16th, seven ironclad river gunboats escorted wooden barges past Vicksburg. Only one transport, the *Henry Clay*, was lost. The transports unloaded their supplies and men at Bruinsburg, 40 miles south of Vicksburg.

Grant made a risky decision. He decided to untether from his supply lines and live off the land. A series of quick battles secured Grant's position deep in hostile territory. On May 12 Grant's advancing forces defeated a small Confederate army at the Battle of Raymond. Victorious Union soldiers marched into Raymond after the battle and helped themselves to a picnic prepared by citizens to show gratefulness to their Confederate soldiers.

On May 14th, Union forces seized Jackson, the capital of Mississippi after Joseph E. Johnston retreated. Grant destroyed anything of value to the Rebels. Satisfied that he would not be attacked from behind, he pressed on to Vicksburg.

Contrary to Davis' orders, Johnston ordered Pemberton to move east to join his forces. Grant prevented Pemberton from joining Johnston. On May 16th, 32,000 Union troops under General John McClernand intercepted 23,000 Rebels on

Soldiers surrounded the Shirley House with protective dugout shelters.

AUTHOR PHOTO

The Shirley House still stands in Vicksburg National Military Park.

Troops pour into the crater created after Union engineers detonated explosives underneath a Confederate position.

a hill at Sid Champion's farm. A determined General Alvin Hovey drove the Rebels off before a counterattack recaptured the ground. Grant committed reinforcement to the battle, eventually driving off the Confederates with superior numbers. The Battle of Champion's Hill was a Union victory.

Pemberton made one final stand at Big Black River the following day. This delaying action allowed the majority of the Rebel troops to retreat into the Vicksburg defenses.

Never one to let his enemy rest, Grant ordered an assault on the Vicksburg defenses on May 19th. McClernand attacked from the east while James B. McPherson and Sherman attacked from the north. Thick underbrush, steep ravines, imposing defenses, and determined defenders thwarted the assault. The Union suffered 942 casualties compared to only 250 Rebel.

A second, more carefully planned assault commenced on May 22nd. The 2nd Texas watched incredulously as private Thomas H. Higgins, 99th Illinois, miraculously evaded fire while bearing the Stars and Stripes. When Higgins walked up to the Confederate line, instead of shooting him, Rebels captured Higgins. The attack turned into a disaster when McClernand overestimated his hold on two rebel positions and convinced Grant to renew

the attack. Having suffered 3,200 more casualties. Grant decided to starve out the city.

During the next six weeks, Grant kept up a continual bombardment of the city. The citizens of Vicksburg dug and lived in caves in the Mississippi bluffs. Hunger set in as soldiers and citizens turned to horse and mule meat. Cats and dogs were soon nowhere to be found.

Both armies sweltered in the unrelenting heat as they worked to improve their positions. On June 25th, Union engineers detonated explosives under a Confederate position. Having heard digging sounds, Confederate soldiers had retreated to an interior line. Federal troops met fierce resistance as they entered the crater and were forced back to their original lines.

By the end of June, Rebel rations were one biscuit and a small amount of bacon each day. Grant planned another attack for July 6th. Pemberton accepted the fact that Johnston was not coming to the rescue. His men too weak to attempt a breakout, Pemberton opened talks with Grant on July 3rd and officially surrendered on Independence Day.

John Pemberton

Union troops treated Vicksburg's civilians and soldiers with kindness, sharing food and refraining from wild celebrations. Grant allowed Pemberton's men to disarm and walk home. The North, already celebrating victory at Gettysburg the previous day, embraced the news with great joy.

EASTERN THEATER

Having secured the Mississippi River, Grant was sent to Chattanooga, Tennessee, to pull the Union out of a mess. Grant drove the Rebels off nearby Lookout Mountain and into Georgia. After Chattanooga, Grant was promoted to Lieutenant General—the highest rank in the Army. Lincoln then brought Grant to Virginia to deal

President Ulysses S. Grant posed for this official portrait by Henry Ulke.

with Robert E. Lee. Grant's plan was simple: grind Lee down with the Union's more numerous forces.

Lee learned quickly that Grant was different from most Union generals. Grant kept up the pressure on Lee despite heavy losses at Spotsylvania, Cold Harbor, and elsewhere. Grant cornered Lee's dwindling forces at Petersburg, Virginia, during the summer of 1864. Settling into a siege, both sides constructed trenches similar to those that would characterize the First World War.

Lee led a successful breakout attempt in April 1865. However, he was unable to join up with Johnston's army. Lee was compelled to surrender to Grant at Appomattox Court House on April 9, 1865. Acting on President Lincoln's order to be-gin the healing of the nation, Grant provided rations for Lee's men and allowed them to go home with their horses.

WAR HERO AND PRESIDENT

In 1866, a grateful nation celebrated Grant's promotion to full general, the first since George Washington. In 1868, Grant succeeded Andrew Johnson as the 18th President of the United States. He was a better soldier than politician. His advisors embroiled the government in fraud and scandal.

In 1884, Grant learned that he had throat cancer. It was the result of a cigar-smoking habit he had formed during the war, Grant wrote his memoirs, finishing just days before his death on July 23, 1885. The memoirs were a huge financial success sorely needed by his family.

In 1897, Grant's remains were moved to a special mausoleum constructed in his honor beside the Hudson River in New York City. William Sherman summed up Grant when he wrote, "Thank God … that we have in Grant not a 'great man' or 'hero' but a good, plain, sensible kind-hearted fellow."

A line of battleships pass Grant's tomb in 1919.

David Dixon Porter

Union Admiral
Born: June 8, 1813
Died: February 13, 1891

Naval hero David Dixon Porter helped lead the Union to victory not on the high seas but along the coasts and on the rivers. Born in Chester, Pennsylvania in 1813, He was the son of Commodore David Porter and adoptive brother of another Famous Man, David Farragut.

David's naval career began at the age of 10 when he sailed with his father to the West Indies. He joined the Mexican Navy at age 12 when his father took command of their navy. David was wounded, captured, and imprisoned in Cuba after a daring raid against larger Spanish ships while serving aboard the 22-gun *Guerrero*. He was later exchanged and sent back to the United States

Porter began a long association with the U.S. Navy at the age of 16. He continued the naval family tradition by marrying the daughter of Commodore Daniel Patterson. Three of the couple's four sons entered the Navy, and both daughters married military officers.

In 1855, Porter commanded the USS *Supply* in purchasing and transporting camels from the Mediterranean for Jefferson Davis' U.S. Camel Corps. When the Civil War began, he was preparing to take command of an uncompleted Pacific mail steamship

Porter responded to the call to preserve the Union. His first mission was to deliver men and supplies to besieged Fort Sumter in South Carolina. Due to confusion in orders, he instead went to Fort Pickens at Pensacola. As a result, the Confederate victory was made easier at Sumter.

Commander Porter led a mortar fleet in assisting his brother David with the capture of New Orleans. His 21 smaller boats armed with 13-inch mortars caused little damage but suppressed fire from forts so Farragut could safely move past them to New Orleans. It was the first of several key battles along the Mississippi in which Porter would have an important role.

RIVERBOAT IRONCLADS

An important part of Winfield Scott's Anaconda Plan was to wrest control of the Mississippi River from the Rebels. The introduction of ironclad gunboats designed for fighting on unpredictable rivers proved invaluable in that task. The gunboats were designed with broad hulls allowing for operations in shallow water, powerful

THE PHOTOGRAPHIC HISTORY OF THE CIVIL WAR

David Dixon Porter poses on the deck of an unidentified ship.

The USS *Baron DeKalb* (formerly the *St. Louis*) was one of seven City-class ironclad river gunboats designed and built by James Buchanan Eads.

The City-class ironclad USS *Cairo* was found entombed in mud in the Yazoo River in 1956. Today, the ship is on display at its own museum in Vicksburg National Military Park.

engines capable of moving against the current, and tough exteriors that could take abuse from enemy shells and overhanging trees.

The need for gunboats became apparent after the outbreak of the war. James Buchanan Eads was tasked with building seven ironclad riverboats. The City-class gunboats, as they were known, were built in St. Louis, Missouri, and Mound City, Illinois, along the Mississippi and Ohio rivers. These first ironclads predated the USS *Monitor* that sailed to fame in the Eastern Theater. The City-class ships were named the *Cairo, Carondelet, Cincinnati, Louisville,*

James Buchanan Eads

Mound City, Pittsburg, and *St. Louis* (later renamed the *Baron DeKalb*).

The *Cairo* assisted in the capture of Fort Pillow. It was sunk by a remotely-detonated mine during the Yazoo Pass Expedition. It was quickly buried in mud, preserving the ship and its many artifacts. Forgotten for decades, it was rediscovered in 1956 and raised in three pieces in 1964. Today, the Cairo is restored and on display at Vicksburg National Military Park.

VICKSBURG CAMPAIGN

In 1863, Porter assumed command of the Western Gunboat Flotilla. Previously under control of the army, the flotilla was a veteran of battles at Fort Henry, Fort Donelson, Island No. 10, and Fort Pillow. The flotilla was

U.S. NAVAL ACADEMY MUSEUM

Admiral Porter's fleet passes Vicksburg on the night of April 16, 1863. The Union ships pictured from front are the *Benton, Lafayette, General Price, Louisville, Mound City, Pittsburg, Carondelet,* transports *Silver Wave, Forest Queen, Henry Clay,* and *Tuscumbia.*

renamed the Mississippi River Squadron and transferred to Porter's command. Porter was promoted to rear admiral, skipping the ranks of captain and commodore.

The squadron supported General John Mc-Clernand in the capture of Fort Hindman on the Arkansas River. The fort was used as a base for raids on the Mississippi and was used to protect Little Rock, Arkansas. It was a four-sided earthen fortification on a bluff manned by about 5000 Arkansas troops and dismounted Texas cavalry. Its existence threatened any Federal movements against Vicksburg.

John McClernand

McClernand enlisted General William Sherman's troops to create a force of 33,000 to attack Fort Hindman. Porter's gunboats *Baron DeKalb, Louisville,* and *Cincinnati* pounded the fort, but the lightly armored tin-clad *Rattler* ran aground and was pummeled by fire from the fort. After a two-day battle, the Union's superior numbers overwhelmed the Rebels' superior position. The result was the largest surrender of Rebel troops west of the Mississippi during the war.

After several Union attempts to approach Vicksburg from the north failed, Porter conceived of a plan to move transports and supplies downriver past the resistant city. This would allow Grant to move troops from the west side of the river to begin the campaign.

On April 16, 1863, a fleet of ironclads and wooden transports made a dash past Vicksburg while taking heavy fire from 50 siege guns and artillery pieces trained on the river. The fleet included the ironclads *Carondelet, Pittsburg, Louisville, Mound City, Tuscumbia, Lafayette,* and *Benton.* Each transport was lashed to the side of an ironclad facing away from the bluffs. The wooden transports had wet cotton bales stacked along their sides and around their steam engines to provide extra protection.

Though it took several hours for all the ships to pass, the only loss was the transport *Henry Clay.* No men were killed and only 12 were wounded.

RED RIVER EXPEDITION

In 1864, the Union still lacked a presence in the Rebel state of Texas and was seeking a source of cotton for northern factories. The urgency of the situation increased when France

FRANK LESLIE'S SCENES AND PORTRAITS OF THE CIVIL WAR

Porter's gunboats pass through Bailey's dam near Alexandria, Louisiana during the Red River Expedition.

THE PHOTOGRAPHIC HISTORY OF THE CIVIL WAR

Admiral David Dixon Porter (center) poses with his staff in 1864.

sent troops to Mexico on the pretext of collecting unpaid debt. French leader Napoleon III installed Maximilian of Habsburg as monarch, and soon French cavalry was patrolling along the Rio Grande River.

Rear Admiral David Porter sent his river gunboats up the Red River through Louisiana to support an advance by General Nathaniel Banks and General Andrew J. Smith. The goal was to capture Shreveport, Louisiana, the gateway to Texas. From that point, cotton could be shipped back to New Orleans and a military campaign could be launched into Texas.

Banks began his march with 17,000 troops, while Smith had about 10,000 under his command. The campaign experienced initial success as Confederate General Kirby Smith traded land for time while consolidating his troops at Shreveport. Low water levels negated the Federal's advantage in firepower as Porter's large gunboats could not pass rapids near Alexandria.

As Banks continued to slowly move north, General Richard Taylor seized an opportunity as the Union column spread out near Mansfield, Louisiana. Though outnumbered, Taylor was able to roll up the flanks of two of Banks' divisions before being stopped by a third. Union forces suffered 2800 casualties compared to just 1000 Confederate casualties. The attack convinced Banks that the campaign was futile. Union soldiers began the long retreat to southern Louisiana.

The Battle of Mansfield would be one of the last great Confederate victories. However, the Rebels failed to destroy Banks' army and Porter's fleet. This would have created the possibility of recapturing New Orleans and bottling up the Mississippi River. Perhaps General William T. Sherman's famous March to the Sea would have taken place in Louisiana rather than Georgia.

LATER YEARS

Porter finished the war in command of the North Atlantic Blockading Squadron. Fort Fisher, a huge fort near Wilmington, North Carolina, protected the last southern port open to blockade runners. General Benjamin Butler assaulted the fort in December 1864 with support from Porter's ships. Butler's plan was to load the USS *Louisiana* with gunpowder and ram the fort. The spectacular explosion had little effect, and Butler aborted the attack.

Angry at Butler's timidity, Porter convinced Grant to replace Butler. In January 1865, Porter sent 2,000 marines to assist General Alfred Terry in capturing the fort and shutting off the Confederacy from the outside world.

Shorty after the war's end, David was appointed Superintendent of the U.S. Naval Academy. There, he reformed the curriculum to better reflect naval life, enforced discipline, and created an honor system. In 1870, he was promoted to admiral as the senior officer of the navy. He spent the following years in semi-retirement writing histories and fictional books. Dixon never regained his health after an 1890 heart attack and died at age 77 in 1891.

Porter played an invaluable role in applying naval power efficiently to control the waterways and cripple southern commerce. For his contributions, he earned the thanks of Congress four times and a place on among the Famous Men.

James Longstreet

**Confederate General
Born: January 8, 1821
Died: January 2, 1904**

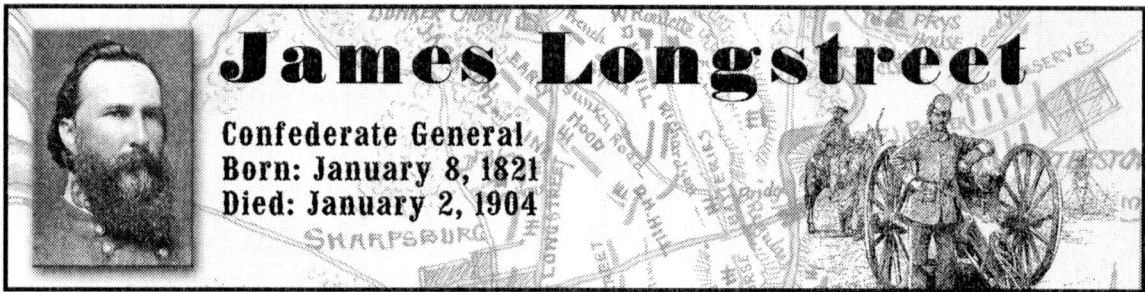

One of the South's most well-known generals, James Longstreet served in almost every major battle in the Eastern Theater. He was also one of the most polarizing figures of the war. General Robert E. Lee fondly called him "My Old Warhorse." However, Longstreet's criticism of his subordinates and Lee, association with several Confederate failures, and postwar support of Reconstruction overshadowed his accomplishments. Many Southerners blamed him for the outcome of the "Lost Cause."

General James Longstreet poses in his Confederate uniform.

Longstreet was born in South Carolina to a farming family. At the age of nine he went to live with his uncle Augustus Longstreet in anticipation of preparing for a military career. At West Point, he befriended officers such as Ulysses S. Grant and George E. Pickett with whom his name is forever linked. He struggled academically, graduating 54th out of 56 cadets in the class of 1842.

During the Mexican-American War, Longstreet was wounded by a musket ball at Chapultepec. He later participated in the Indian Wars and was serving in the New Mexico territory as a paymaster when the Civil War began. A supporter of states' rights, he volunteered to serve as paymaster general of the Confederate Army. Instead, President Jefferson Davis gave him command of an infantry brigade.

Longstreet's brigade thwarted an attempt by Union forces to advance across Blackburn Creek in one of the first direct engagements of the war. His coolness under fire earned the respect of his men and quick promotion to major general after the First Battle of Bull Run. He fought a delaying action during the Peninsula Campaign that allowed Confederate troops to retreat from Yorktown and defend Richmond.

Longstreet's many struggles began on a deeply personal level. While he was engaged in the Peninsula Campaign, three of his young children died of scarlet fever. He also endured criticism for the Confederate disaster at the Battle of Seven Pines. General Joseph E. Johnston gave oral commands to Longstreet during a long meeting shortly before the battle. Longstreet either misunderstood or changed the orders. As a result, Longstreet's men were delayed and only a fraction participated in battle.

BATTLES AND LEADERS OF THE CIVIL WAR

Union soldiers flee the field aftr defeat at the Second Battle of Bull Run.

The failure at Seven Pines was forgotten after success at the Second Battle of Bull Run. Longstreet expertly coordinated his 28,000 men in a counterattack that crushed the Union left flank. Victory in this battle stabilized the defense of Virginia and convinced Lee to take the battle to Union soil.

ANTIETAM

Emboldened by George McClellan's retreat from Richmond, Lee invaded the North late in the summer of 1862. His goals were to demoralize northerners by threatening Washington, D.C, and to seize much-needed supplies. Stonewall Jackson and Longstreet forced Union General John Pope's battered forces to retreat within the formidable Washington, D.C. defenses.

Lee's troops crossed into Maryland on September 4, 1862. He issued Order Number 191 sending half of his army to the rail center of Harrisburg, Pennsylvania. The other half were sent under Jackson's command to capture weapons factories at Harper's Ferry.

A copy of the order dropped by rebel troops moving northward was found by a Union soldier. The precious intelligence was soon in McClellan's hands. This fortunate turn of events revealed that Lee had only 40,000 men compared to McClel-

LIBRARY OF CONGRESS

This fanciful illustration shows the struggle for Burnside's Bridge at Antietam on September 17, 1862.

Bloody Lane as it appears today at Antietam National Battlefield.

lan's 76,000. Refusing to believe his good fortune, McClellan continued to make decisions as if he were outnumbered.

Lee deployed his troops into a defensive line along Antietam Creek east of Sharpsburg, Maryland. In response, McClellan launched three uncoordinated attacks on the morning of September 17th. General Joseph Hooker drove back the Rebel left flank until Lee ordered in reinforcements that shattered Hooker's corps.

The Union XII Corps followed up by disordering Confederate lines near Dunkard Church before being pushed back. A division of II Corps under Edwin "Bull" Sumner appeared likely to roll up the weak Confederate flank. Lee ordered in two more divisions,

George McClellan

turning the tide of battle and nearly annihilating Sumner's corps.

At midday, the battle shifted to the center. Longstreet's troops held the center at a sunken road that became known as "Bloody Lane." Eventually, the greater Union numbers pushed the Rebels back to Sharpsburg. A war correspondent seeing the carnage at Bloody Lane said, "... Confederates had gone down as the grass falls before a scythe." McClellan did not send available reserves into the Rebel center that was ripe for destruction.

On the Union left, General Ambrose Burnside concentrated his efforts on capturing a stone bridge. A determined charge by Burnside's troops established a foothold on the other side. Soon Union troops streamed across the bridge. Burnside might have cut off Lee's retreat, but General A.P. Hill's troops arrived from Harper's Ferry in time to create a stalemate. McClellan again held

THE BATTLE OF ANTIETAM
September 17, 1862
Maryland

Potomac River

Meade
Doubleday
Mansfield
Franklin
Stuart
Rickets
Early
McLaws
Sumner
Bloody Lane
Hood
JACKSON
Pleasonton
Porterstown
McCLELLAN
D. H. Hill
Porter
Sharpsburg
LEE
D.R. Jones
Burnside
Toombs
Burnside Bridge
LONGSTREET
A.P. Hill
Antietam Creek

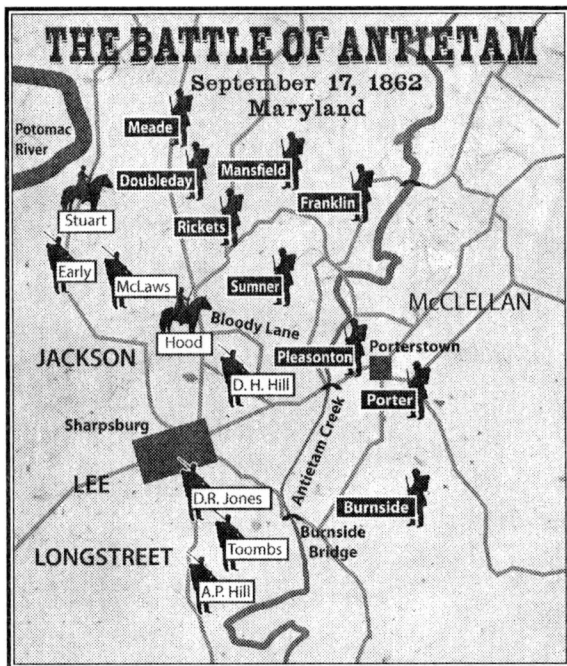

a corps in reserve that might have turned the battle into a rout.

Lee held his position overnight in anticipation of McClellan, renewing the attack in the morning. McClellan received two more divisions but, ever hesitant, did not renew the battle. With the way forward blocked, Lee retreated to Virginia. The cautious McClellan failed to pursue.

Antietam is regarded as a Union success but also as a lost opportunity to destroy Lee's army. The Army of the Potomac was motivated not to suffer the shame of yet another loss. It succeeded in stopping Lee and the Army of North Virginia for the first time.

Antietam had broad political ramifications. The battle convinced European countries that the South was not in position to win the war. They withheld support. Lincoln took advantage of the victory to announce the Emancipation Proclamation. Ending slavery became a stated objective of the Union war effort.

The haunting legacy of Antietam is as the bloodiest single-day battle in American history.

More than 23,000 men were killed or wounded on that fateful day.

LATER CAMPAIGNS

Longstreet was promoted to Lieutenant General after the Sharpsburg Campaign. His promotion and the death of Stonewall Jackson combined to his becoming one of Lee's most trusted generals.

Longstreet continually argued that the South should wage only a defensive war. During the Battle of Fredericksburg, he put his defensive knowledge into organizing the defense of Marye's Heights. The Union attempt to capture the heights was an utter failure.

Emboldened by success at Fredericksburg, Lee planned an invasion of Pennsylvania. Lee ordered Longstreet's troops to attack the Union left flank late on the second day. Longstreet's men suffered high casualties in an attack that nearly succeeded.

The next day, over Longstreet's vigorous protests, Lee ordered an attack against the Union center. One of three divisions under Longstreet's command was led by General Pickett. The destruction of Pickett's division while approaching the Union lines was the defining moment of the Confederate defeat at Gettysburg. Longstreet's official report condemned Lee's order:

"The distance to be passed over under fire of the enemy's batteries, and in plain view, seemed too great to insure great results...The order for this attack, which I could not favor under better auspices, would have been revoked if I had that privilege."

In the fall of 1863, Longstreet moved to the Western Theater. He arrived in time to help General Braxton Bragg to victory at Chickamauga. Bragg and Longstreet had a dislike for one another, so Bragg sent him to recapture Knoxville, Tennessee. The short campaign resulted in a bungled assault, exposing Longstreet's weakness as an independent commander. He alien-

Union line on Cemetery Hill

Rebel starting position

Rebel lines march across a wide expanse in this painting by Edwin Forbes depicting the ill-fated Pickett's Charge at Gettysburg.

ated many Southerners by blaming his subordinates for failure.

Longstreet returned to the Army of North Virginia in April 1864. During the Battle of the Wilderness he was accidentally injured by his own soldiers in the same way and near the same spot as Stonewall Jackson one year before. A Minié ball passed through his neck and shoulder, rendering his right arm paralyzed.

After recovery, he defended railroads leading into Richmond in the final days of the war. He was present with Lee at Appomattox.

BITTERNESS AFTER THE WAR

Southerners made Longstreet a scapegoat for the defeat, contrasting him with Lee and Jackson whom they worshipped. Longstreet continued to give critics reasons to attack him.

In 1867, Longstreet went on record as supporting Reconstruction. He joined the Republican Party and supported U.S. Grant in his 1868 presidential campaign. Grant appointed him as Surveyor of Customs for the Port of New Or-

leans. This close association with the Union's greatest general further upset Southerners.

Longstreet's worst crime was continuing his criticism of Lee and other officers. Many southern generals and leaders came to Lee's defense.

Longstreet's men took a better view of him, inviting him to veteran meetings and monument dedications well into the 1890s. Decades after the war, he published his memoirs, *From Manassas to Appomattox*, defending his war record. After the death of his wife, Longstreet married a much younger woman, Helen Dortch, in 1897. Longstreet died in 1904 shortly before his 93rd birthday. His wife continued to defend his reputation until her death in 1962.

Widely criticized as a poor general when given independent command, Longstreet excelled as a corps commander and tactician. Whatever personal feelings Southerners and historians might have about Longstreet, he earns a place as a Famous Man for his prominent role in numerous important Civil War engagements.

Ambrose Everett Burnside

Union General
Born: May 23, 1824
Died: September 13, 1881

Few Famous Men have struck as imposing a figure as Ambrose Burnside. A tall man with a large forehead, Burnside's most recognizable feature was his carefully manicured whiskers which to this day are called "sideburns" in his honor. He was a well-liked and friendly person who always remembered others' names. His Civil War career is a cautionary tale of what can happen when one is promoted beyond one's abilities.

Burnside was born to a farming family of Scottish heritage in Indiana. Originally apprenticed to a tailor, Burnside was able to secure an appointment to West Point. Shortly after graduation in 1847, he served in garrison duty during the Mexican-American War.

Resigning his commission in 1853, Burnside went into a private venture developing the "Burnside carbine" for the U.S. Army. The venture failed when a large government contract was revoked. His West Point friend, George McClellan, secured him a job as treasurer of the Illinois Central Railroad.

EARLY WAR SUCCESS

Burnside organized the 1st Rhode Island Infantry right after the war began. It was one of the first units to reach and defend Washington, D.C., in the uncertain early days of the war. He commanded his brigade at First Bull Run.

In September 1861, he was given command of three brigades making up the North

Burnside's Bridge at Antietam National Battlefield is well-maintained.

The Army of the Potomac attempts to cross the Rappahannock River and enter Fredericksburg, Virginia.

Carolina Expeditionary Force. Success in establishing a foothold on Roanoke Island and the North Carolina coast led to a promotion to major general.

Burnside's experience working with smaller units did not carry over at Antietam, where he struggled to command the large Union I and IX Corps. Instead of fording Antietam Creek at several nearby low spots, Burnside concentrated his forces on a lengthy and costly struggle for a single bridge.

After Antietam, President Abraham Lincoln sought to replace McClellan with Burnside as commander of the Army of the Potomac. Understanding his limits, Burnside turned down the offer to replace his friend twice before accepting the third time.

FREDERICKSBURG

Under political pressure to act, Burnside ignored the conventional wisdom of avoiding winter warfare. In November 1862, he planned to use pontoon boats to cross the Rappahannock River in a surprise move to capture Fredericksburg, Virginia. A delay in the delivery of boats allowed General Robert E. Lee to maneuver his forces to Fredericksburg.

Union engineers finally began building the bridge on December 11, 1862. Confederate General William Barksdale posted sharpshooters to harass Union soldiers working on the exposed bridge. Burnside sent infantry across the river in boats, while under fire, to establish a bridgehead. Hand-to-hand fighting against the Rebel rearguard in Fredericksburg and subsequent looting of buildings by Union soldiers led to further delays. If Burnside had managed to get more men over on the 11th, maintained discipline, and attacked the next day, the outcome of the impending battle might have been different.

The delays in Fredericksburg allowed Lee and his subordinates, Stonewall Jackson and James Longstreet, to prepare strong defenses on the high ground overlooking the Rappahannock Valley. Burnside launched two attacks on December 13th. The plan was to pin Longstreet's men on the northern end of line at Marye's Heights with one attack. This would prevent Lee from reinforcing Jackson along the southern end of the Rebel line at Prospect Hill where Burnside planned to simultaneously launch the main assault.

Jackson had just 37,000 troops to oppose Burnside's 65,000. However, Burnside's poorly written orders failed to make his plans clear to General William B. Franklin. As a result, Franklin only committed 8000 men in two divisions led by George Meade and John Gibbon. The two divisions advanced across an empty field that became known as the slaughter pen.

THE PHOTOGRAPHIC HISTORY OF THE CIVIL WAR

General Burnside surveys a battlefield in 1862.

In spite of heavy artillery fire from the hill and the need to cross a swampy ditch fence, Meade's Pennsylvania men were able to penetrate Jackson's lines by early afternoon. Both sides ran out of ammunition and began fighting hand-to-hand. Jackson's men rallied and pushed Meade's men back. Union artillery cut down many of the Rebels pursuing Meade's retreating force into the slaughter pen.

John Gibbon

Gibbon attacked General Ambrose P. Hill's troops entrenched behind a railroad embankment. After two failed assaults, Gibbon's men captured the railroad and drove the Rebels into a marsh. The rebels counterattacked, repulsing Gibbon's men. The Union suffered 5000 casu-

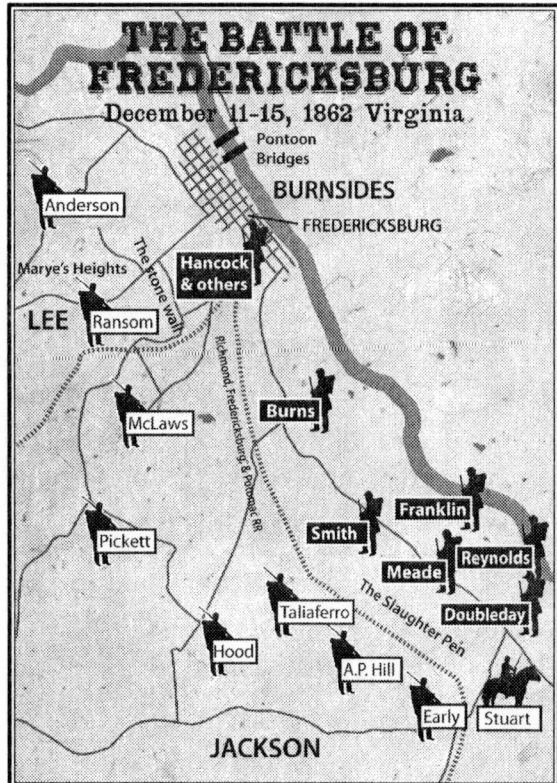

THE BATTLE OF FREDERICKSBURG
December 11-15, 1862 Virginia

BATTLES AND LEADERS OF THE CIVIL WAR

Confederate soldiers fire on exposed Federal troops while taking advantage of protection afforded by a stone wall on Marye's Heights.

alties in the failed attempt to take Prospect Hill. The South suffered 4000 casualties.

Even though it was a secondary attack, Fredericksburg is remembered for the tragic Union attack at Marye's Heights. Believing that Lee had weakened his defenses to support the fighting to the south, Burnside ordered a direct assault against Marye's Heights. The Rebels not only had a clear advantage in elevation but were protected by a sunken road behind a stone wall. In addition, Union troops had to cross a large ditch and then cover 500 yards uphill just to reach the wall.

During the course of the day, 17 Union brigades resolutely attempted—and failed—to capture the heights. No Union soldier got within 30 yards of the wall. As darkness fell that evening, soldiers found themselves pinned on the field

amidst—thousands of dead and seriously wounded comrades—by Rebel sharpshooters. Moved by the scene, Lee said to Longstreet, "It is well that war is so terrible, or we would grow too fond of it."

Lieutenant Daniel George McNamara of the 9th Massachusetts had this to say of Fredericksburg:

> "The rebel position was unassailable; it was a perfect slaughter-pen, and column after column was broken against it. Our artillery did so little injury to the enemy that they were able to concentrate all their fire on the advancing columns of troops."

The foolish assault cost the Union another 8000 casualties. In contrast, the rebels only suffered 1000 casualties at Marye's Heights. Amazingly, Burnside had to be talked out of renewing the attack the next day. The Army of the Potomac recrossed the Rappahannock, leaving Fredericksburg to the Rebels. Lee felt that he had been denied a complete victory by Burnside's retreat.

The defeat at Fredericksburg created a time of dread and mourning in the North. Burnside took responsibility for the debacle, but ultimately the battle had little strategic impact. The Army of the Potomac (AotP) would regroup and eventually defeat Lee in 1865.

THE BATTLE OF THE CRATER

A month after Fredericksburg, Burnside resigned after clashing with disgruntled subordinates. Lincoln appointed Joseph Hooker to lead the Army of the Potomac and transferred Burnside to command of the Department and Army of Ohio. Burnside excelled in commanding the smaller army, repulsing John Hunt Morgan's raid in Ohio and later holding Knoxville against an assault by James Longstreet.

In January 1864, Burnside resumed command of IX Corps in the AotP in the Eastern Theater. His military career ended during the Petersburg Campaign after he was blamed for failure at the Battle of the Crater.

Soldiers of the 48th Pennsylvania who had coal mining experience dug a tunnel under Confederate lines near Petersburg and packed it with 8000 pounds of gunpowder. George Meade, the current commander of the AotP, rejected Burnside's plan to use a colored division that had received training to exploit the breach after the explosion. Instead, Burnside had his three commanders chose lots to see whose men would lead the assault. The "winner" was General James Ledlie's division. Ledlie failed to instruct his men and was later found out to have been drinking behind lines during the battle.

Shortly before dawn on July 30th, a great explosion sent shockwaves across the battlefield. The explosion immediately killed 278 Rebels and created a crater 170 feet wide and 30 feet

NATIONAL PARK SERVICE

The Petersburg battlefield resembled a moonscape after the Battle of the Crater.

deep. Ledlie's soldiers poured into the crater, rather than around it as planned. Trapped, they were easily mowed down. Almost 1900 Union soldiers were killed as a result of the poorly executed attack.

Though Ledlie was dismissed, Burnside received most of the criticism for the defeat. Meade censured Burnside, but a later inquiry in 1865 absolved Burnside of blame and instead blamed Meade for carelessly altering the battle plan. Regardless, Burnside was not given another command.

RAILROAD MAN AND POLITICIAN

Burnside found success in civilian life after the war. He worked as president for three different railroads and served as Governor of Rhode Island. During an 1870 trip to Europe, he attempted to mediate between France and Germany in the Franco-Prussian War. He spent the last seven years of his life as a senator from Rhode Island.

A heart condition led to Burnside's unexpected death in 1881. He was buried in Rhode Island. Ambrose Burnside was a patriot who loyally served his state and country. He was not burdened with the arrogance that many Union generals exhibited. However, he goes down in history as a general who was promoted beyond his ability and was incapable of leading a large army.

Thomas Jonathan "Stonewall" Jackson

Confederate General
Born: January 21, 1824
Died: May 10, 1863

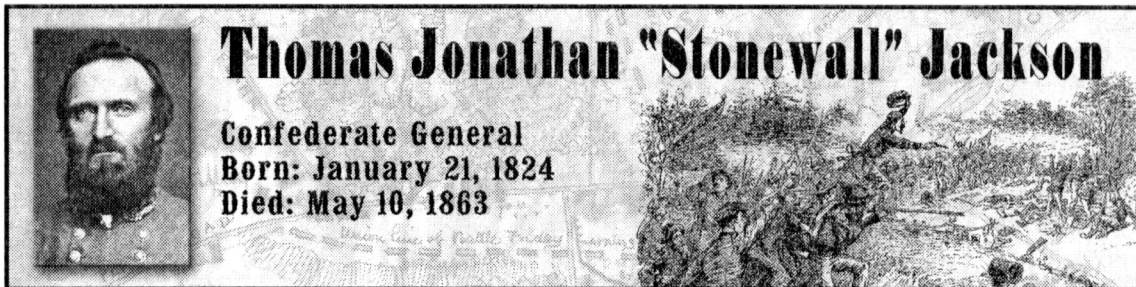

Many Americans recognize the Famous Man with the name "Stonewall" Jackson. The Scotch-Irish descendant was born Thomas Jonathan Jackson in Clarksburg, Virginia. His father died when Thomas was just three years old and his mother died when he was seven. Thomas lived with extended family members before settling down with his father's half-brother, a farmer.

Jackson's limited schooling did not affect his determination to succeed. Much of what he learned was self-taught through reading. He once taught a slave how to read in exchange for pine knots that Jackson could burn at night to read by.

Thomas was accepted into West Point after amother cadet decided against attending at the last moment. Due to his lack of formal education, Jackson struggled academically and was teased about his modest upbringing. This only served to increase his resolve. His efforts paid off as he graduated 17th of 59 cadets in the class of 1846.

His first assignment was during the Mexican-American War with Winfield Scott's army. During this time, he met his future commander Robert E. Lee.

A deeply spiritual man, Jackson became a follower of Jesus Christ during the Mexican-American War and joined the Presbyterian Church. He gained a reputation as a man who refused to gamble, drink, smoke, or swear. In 1851, he resigned his commission and went to teach at the Virginia Military Institute (VMI).

Jackson hoped that Virginia would remain with the Union, but, he became a strong supporter of secession when the United States required Virginia to raise troops in order to put down the rebellion. He began the war as a colonel of Virginia militia at Harper's Ferry where he organized a brigade and led them to Manassas. He was promoted to brigadier general shortly before the First Battle of Bull Run.

EARLY BATTLES

Jackson's brigade was instrumental in turning the tide of battle at First Bull Run at a critical moment. Jackson endeared himself to his men that day by remaining calm even when exposed to enemy fire. General Barnard Bee was rumored to say, "There is Jackson standing like a stone wall!" The legend of Stonewall Jackson

LIBRARY OF CONGRESS

Stonewall Jackson poses in his Confederate officer's uniform.

This Currier and Ives print depicts a romantic view of the war. It implies a Union victory at the Second Battle of Bull Run, which it was not.

was born, and he became a southern celebrity overnight. Jackson's brigade earned respect as the Stonewall Brigade.

Though a hero in the eyes of the people of the South, Jackson had low moments. In January 1862 General William Loring refused to follow Jackson's command to capture Romney, Virginia. Loring appealed to the secretary of war who rescinded the orders. Angry, Jackson offered his resignation stating that he would not tolerate interference with his command. His resignation was refused.

Jackson lost a battle at Kernstown. He blamed it on intelligence that suggested Union forces were fewer and as a result of violating Sunday as a Christian day of rest. A number of losses during the Peninsula Campaign marred his record but did not ruin his reputation.

SECOND BULL RUN

In July 1862, President Abraham Lincoln approved a plan to unite the three separate armies in the Eastern Theater under a single commander, John Pope. Lee sent forces under Jackson and James Longstreet to intercept Pope before he could unite the armies. Jackson captured a Union depot at Manassas in August and deployed a strong defensive line.

John Pope

Even though Pope's troops outnumbered Jackson's about 60,000 to 20,000, poorly planned movements scattered Pope's army and Jackson was able to repel the attacks. The next day, Pope launched new attacks but was nearly enveloped by Jack-

Soldiers survey the debris of the Henry Hill house after the Second Battle of Bull Run.

son's army. A delaying action at the Henry House Hill allowed Pope's troops to escape back to Washington.

Second Bull Run was a transition point as growing confidence encouraged Lee to move from the defensive to the offensive. However, heavy losses on both sides began to reveal a Confederate weakness that could not be fixed— the Union could replace losses while the South could not.

Jackson played an important role at the Battle of Antietam in September 1862 by quickly marching his men to help save Lee's army. The use of swiftly moving infantry as "foot cavalry" became a trademark of Jackson's strategic movements.

TRIVIA

Stonewall Jackson apparently suffered from the sleeping disorder narcolepsy. As a result, he fell asleep at inconvenient times, including while eating.

Stonewall commanded II Corps at Fredericksburg in December 1862. He arranged cannons on Prospect Hill overlooking the Rappahannock Valley. From this vantage point, he was able to decimate the Union I Corps as it crossed an open field remembered thereafter as the Slaughter Pen.

THE CHANCELLORSVILLE CAMPAIGN

As a result of the debacle at Fredericksburg, Lincoln replaced Burnside with Joseph Hooker as commander of the Army of the Potomac (AotP) in January 1863. Lee's 60,000 troops spent the winter camped opposite Hooker's 130,000 Federals along the Rappahannock River.

In late April, Hooker split his army in an attempt to trap Lee with a pincer movement. The plan was for one half to hold Lee at Fredericksburg while the other would cross 40 miles upstream beyond the Confederate defenses. Hooker said with great confidence, "My plans are perfect, and

Joseph Hooker

when I start to carry them out may God have mercy on General Lee, for I will have none."

Discerning Hooker's intentions, Lee decided to attack Hooker's western element while leaving just 10,000 men to hold Fredericksburg. The two sides met in early May 1863 at Chancellorsville, a crossroads with a tavern located 10 miles west of Fredericksburg in a tangled woods known as the Wilderness.

Hooker halted at the tavern to await more troops. This delay proved disastrous. The troops of Confederate Generals Richard H. Anderson and Lafayette McLaws were preparing defensive works near Chancellorsville when Stonewall Jackson arrived. Jackson ordered the division to prepare for attack. When the order was given to move eastward out of the Wilderness, Hooker's troops were rudely greeted by

Stonewall Jackson rides with two of his officers.

the Rebels. Rather than overwhelm the outnumbered Confederates, the startled Union troops returned to Chancellorsville and took up defensive positions.

At a campfire conference that night, J.E.B. Stuart reported to Lee and Jackson that the Federal right flank was "up in the air" and not resting on an obstacle. Armed with this intelligence, Lee decided to take one of the great gambles of the war. Having already split his army once, Lee detached Jackson and his 30,000 men to make a 12-mile forced march along back roads and paths to surprise the Federal right. Lee would distract Hooker with his 14,000 remaining troops.

Union troops spotted Jackson's column more than once, but Hooker interpreted the movements as a retreat. Scattered reports of Rebels silently gathering in the woods near the Federal left flank were dismissed as alarmist.

At about 5:00 pm, Oliver O. Howard's XI Corps was settling down for dinner. The hungry Yankees were shocked as the sound of bugles and yells preceded a two-mile wide line of Rebels running out of the woods. The battle quickly became a rout.

As darkness descended over the battlefield, the two sides became intermingled. Jackson met with A.P. Hill and decided to regroup and press the attack. Stonewall hoped to cut off Hooker's escape route across the river and then, with Lee's help from the opposite direction, destroy the Federal army.

While scouting, Stonewall's party was mistaken by the 18th North Carolina regiment for Union soldiers. Jackson was hit three times in the volley. Hill was injured a short time later. Command fell to Stuart, who prudently called off the night attack.

The day after Jackson's stunning victory in the Wilderness, Union General John Sedgwick's troops managed to dislodge General Jubal Early's troops from Marye's Heights. Sedgwick avoided Burnside's previous mistakes by ordering his troops to press the attack using bayonets rather than stopping to fire. Lee's reinforcements stopped Sedgewick from meeting up with Hooker at the Battle of Salem Church. Hooker ordered his army to recross the Rappahannock, and the Chancellorsville Campaign came to an end.

Union soldiers rest before the Second Battle of Fredericksburg.

Stonewall Jackson leads a camp prayer meeting. Many revival meetings were held in Union and Confederate camps. As a result, thousands of soldiers converted to Christianity during the war.

THE DEATH
OF STONEWALL JACKSON

The AotP would live to fight another day. The same could not be said for Jackson. The next morning, Jackson's left arm was amputated. Lee sent Jackson a note saying, "Could I have directed events, I should have chosen, for the good of the country, to have been disabled in your stead. I congratulate you upon the victory, which is due to your skill and energy." Jackson responded, "General Lee should give the praise to God." Lee also lamented,, "You are better off than I am, for while you have only lost your LEFT, I have lost my RIGHT arm."

Battle wounds would not kill Jackson directly. He developed pneumonia and his strength began to fade. Jackson's final words reflected his faith that there is a better place beyond this world: "Let us cross over the river, and rest under the shade of the trees." He was survived by his wife and a three-week-old daughter. Stonewall was buried in Lexington, Virginia.

Chancellorsville is widely regarded as Lee's greatest victory. The victory convinced him that the time was right for a second invasion of the North. The result would be a resounding defeat at Gettysburg. How might Gettysburg have gone differently if Stonewall Jackson were still alive? Historians can only speculate.

Winfield Scott Hancock

Union General
Born: February 14, 1824
Died: February 9, 1886

A career soldier, Winfield Scott Hancock's great tactical skills and high standing among his men made him one of the Union's best field commanders. Born at Montgomery Square, Pennsylvania, Hancock was prophetically named after War of 1812 hero and Famous Man Winfield Scott. Showing interest in military training at an early age, Winfield entered West Point at 16.

Hancock's first assignment was with the 6th Infantry at Fort Towson in the Indian Territory. He took part in the four major battles of the Mexican-American War and earned a promotion for bravery. During the war, he fought alongside future Gettysburg opponent James Longstreet.

FRIENDS DIVIDED

Hancock was the chief quartermaster of the Southern District of California when the Civil War began. He invited fellow officers Albert S. Johnston, Lewis Armistead, and Richard Garnett to a dinner he had prepared before the men headed east to serve the Confederacy. He did not agree with Abraham Lincoln's views, but he believed secession was wrong, stating, "My politics are of a practical kind—the integrity of the country, the supremacy of the Federal government, an honorable peace or none at all."

Assuming quartermaster duties after returning east, Hancock was unexpectedly promoted to field command by George Mc-Clellan. His organizational skills and tacti-

LIBRARY OF CONGRESS

Winfield Scott Hancock poses in his officer's uniform.

LIBRARY OF CONGRESS

Union defenders repel an attack on Culp's Hill during the second day of the Battle of Gettysburg.

A view of Gettysburg, Pennsylvania as it appeared in 1863.

cal ability were evident during the Peninsula Campaign, earning him the title Hancock the Superb. His initiative at Williamsburg caught the attention of superiors and led to important roles at Frazier's Farm, South Mountain and Antietam.

Hancock argued against General Ambrose Burnside's ill-fated assault up Marye's Heights at Fredericksburg. However, he dutifully led his men while receiving a wound in the process. In the spring of 1863, he was given command of II Corps of the Army of the Potomac (AotP). He received another wound at the Battle of Chancellorsville.

GETTYSBURG, THE FIRST DAY

In June 1863, a confident General Robert E. Lee crossed the Potomac River and invaded the North via southern Pennsylvania. Lee hoped to force the AotP to meet him in a decisive battle. Victory would strengthen the peace movement in the North and might yet convince European powers to support the South.

Lee divided his forces to seek supplies, sever railroads, and threaten Harrisburg—Pennsylvania's capital. When President Lincoln learned of Lee's movements, he prodded General Joe Hooker to pursue and attack. Sensing Hooker's hesitation, Lincoln promoted Gen-

John Reynolds   Richard Ewell   J.E.B. Stuart   A.P. Hill   Lewis Armistead

Some of the fiercest fighting of the Battle of Gettysburg took place at Devil's Den on the second day.

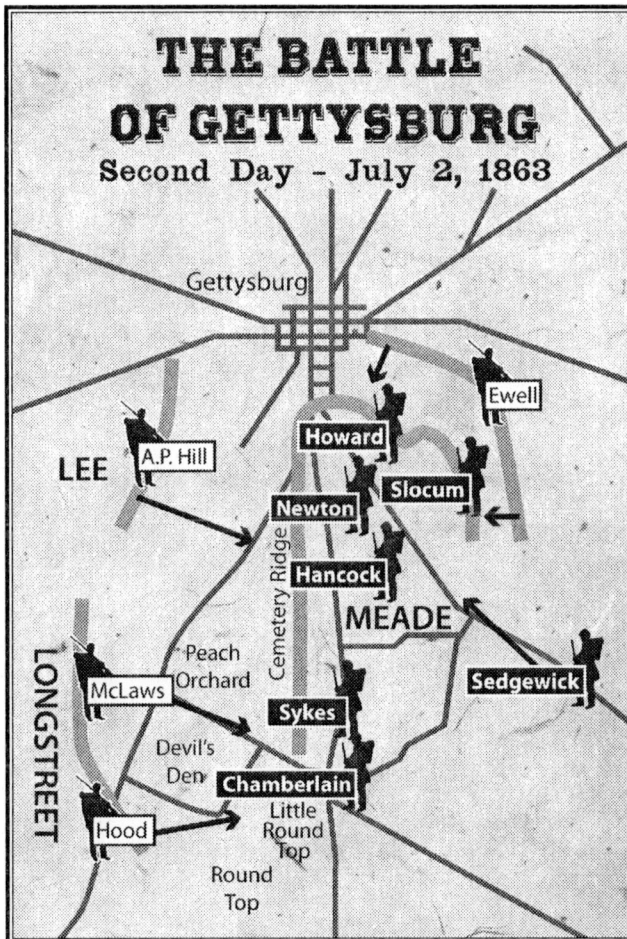

THE BATTLE OF GETTYSBURG
Second Day – July 2, 1863

Gettysburg

Ewell

LEE

A.P. Hill

Howard

Slocum

Newton

Hancock

MEADE

Cemetery Ridge

Peach Orchard

McLaws

Sedgewick

LONGSTREET

Sykes

Devil's Den

Chamberlain

Little Round Top

Hood

Round Top

General George Meade was commander of the Union's Army of the Potomac during the Battle of Gettysburg.

eral George Meade on June 28th to command the AotP.

It was Lee's secondary goal of foraging for much-needed supplies—in this case it was news of a shoe factory—that led to the Civil War's largest battle taking place at Gettysburg. Confederate General A.P. Hill's III Corps was dispatched to search the city, which was strategically located at the intersection of a dozen roads.

Lee had a disadvantage in that his cavalry under J.E.B. Stuart was on a raid, depriving his army of intelligence-gathering capabilities. Hill had no idea that Union troops were also approaching Gettysburg.

The battle commenced on July 1st when two brigades of Union cavalry under John Buford met Hill's men west of Gettysburg. Outnumbered three to one, Buford's men held long enough for the advance elements of John F. Reynolds' I Corps to arrive and bring the Rebel advance to a standstill. Reynolds was killed by a bullet to the head from a sniper.

Lee ordered his scattered troops to rendezvous at Gettysburg. Lee and General Richard Ewell managed to push the Union forces east through town and onto Culp's Hill and Cemetery Ridge. While the first day's fighting appeared to be a Confederate victory, the Union controlled the high ground. Union and Rebel units converged on Gettysburg overnight.

Hancock arrived at dusk, anchoring the Union defenses on Cemetery Ridge with his corps. This was the first of many critical command decisions he would make during the battle.

GETTYSBURG, THE SECOND DAY

As morning broke on July 2nd, Hancock and Meade had arrayed 90,000 men along a fish-hook-shaped three-fourths mile line stretching from Culp's Hill, across Cemetery Ridge, and ending near Little Round Top, a rocky hill to the south. Hancock commanded the left end of the line where Lee would choose to concentrate his attack.

Dan Sickles

General Dan Sickles, commander of the Union III Corps, moved troops off Little Round Top to defend places in front

Rebel lines advance on Little Round Top during the Battle of Gettysburg in this painting by Edwin Forbes.

This painting by Thure de Thulstrup features a view of Pickett's Charge from behind the Union lines. General Hancock (center left) sits on his horse and points.

including the Peach Orchard and Devil's Den, a maze of large rocky outcroppings. Lee ordered James Longstreet's I Corps to break Sickles' line and capture Little Round Top. Longstreet protested because his troops were outnumbered and would have to attack uphill against entrenched troops. He instead encouraged maneuvering between the AotP and Washington, D.C., to force Meade to fight on ground of their choosing. Lee responded, "The enemy is there, and I am going to attack him there."

Longstreet's 15,000 men overran Sickles' troops after intense fighting and rushed to seize the vacated Little Round Top. The 20th Maine, led by school teacher Joshua Chamberlain, was sent double-time to man the crest and hold the end of the line. The 20th Maine expended all of its ammunition, repelling several assaults by Longstreet's 15th Alabama. Chamberlain ordered a bayonet charge that swept the 15th Alabama off the hill and secured the Union flank.

The 1st Minnesota Regiment achieved glory in the center of the Union line. Hancock ordered a desperate attack by the 232 men of the 1st to stall 1600 Rebels until reinforcements arrived. Only 47 of the men returned, but they succeeded in buying time for other units to rein-

James Longstreet

George Pickett

The few Rebels that reached the Union line on Cemetery Ridge during the third day of the Battle of Gettysburg were met by a hail of fire.

force the line. The 82% casualty rate was the highest for any American unit ever in a single day. A third more became casualties the next day during Pickett's charge.

Ewell made an assault late in the day against the Union right at Culp's Hill. The little ground Ewell gained was lost in a Union counterattack at dusk. The Union line had held. Each side lost more than 9000 troops. The 35,000 casualties over two days was already the largest single-battle toll of the war.

GETTYSBURG, THE THIRD DAY

In spite of failures on the second day, Lee believed that the Union army was close to collapse. Meade considered retreating but decided to stay and fight. The results of the third day would dramatically shift the course of the war.

Lee ordered Ewell to attack the Union left and draw off reinforcements from the center, where Lee believed that the Union was weakest. Against Longstreet's continuing protests, Lee ordered him to send three divisions, two under Hill and one under General George Pickett, across an open field against dug-in infantry supported by artillery.

The largest Confederate barrage of the war preceded the advance but did little dam-

age. After the bombardment, 15,000 Rebel soldiers formed a mile-wide line. Stepping out of the woods they advanced across open ground under a hail of Union artillery. As they moved into range, Union soldiers began yelling, "Remember Fredericksburg!" General Armistead and several hundred Virginians and Tennesseans breached the first line but were soon repulsed. The former dinner guests, Garnett and Armistead, were killed near Hancock's position.

The attack faltered and only about half of the Rebels escaped. The disastrous maneuver has been unfairly labeled as Pickett's Charge. Lee retreated, never again to invade the North or mount a major offensive. Any hope of foreign intervention on behalf of the Confederacy evaporated. Lee lost more than a third of his army, 28,000 men. Union losses amounted to 25,000, making Gettysburg the deadliest battle of the war. The AotP finally had its long-awaited great victory, triggering a great celebration in Washington, D.C. on the 4th of July.

General Hancock poses with his staff.

A campaign poster urged voters to support General Hancock in the 1880 U.S. Presidential election.

DUTY TO THE END

A bullet struck Hancock's saddle during Pickett's Charge, driving nails and wood into his leg. He stayed on the field of battle but endured several months of painful recovery afterwards. His name was notably absent from a Joint Resolution of Congress thanking Generals Meade, Hooker, and Oliver O. Howard for their contributions at Gettysburg. Howard, commander of the Union XI Corps, was the senior Union commander on the first day after the death of Reynolds.

Hancock rejoined the AotP in March 1865. He led troops at Spotsylvania and Cold Harbor, as well as at Petersburg where his troops suffered heavy losses due to U.S. Grant's direct tactics. His last battle was at Burgess Mill attempting to cut a supply line to Petersburg. At one point, his forces were surrounded on three sides but managed to repel the attackers. His corps badly mauled, Hancock retreated back to original lines before Rebel reinforcements could arrive.

After the war ended, Hancock was given command over the Department of the Dakota and later the Department of the East. The war hero used his fame and political skill to secure the Democratic nomination for U.S. President in 1880. He lost the general election to James A. Garfield by a narrow margin. He was still commanding the Department of the East when he died in 1886 from complications caused by diabetes.

Even though Grant and Hancock had political disagreements, Grant wrote highly of Hancock:

> *"...his name was never mentioned as having committed a battle blunder for which he was responsible...His genial disposition made him friends, and his personal courage and his presence with his command in the thickest of the fight won for him the confidence of troops serving under him."*

Hancock certainly earned his place among the Famous Men for his balance of command and people skills.

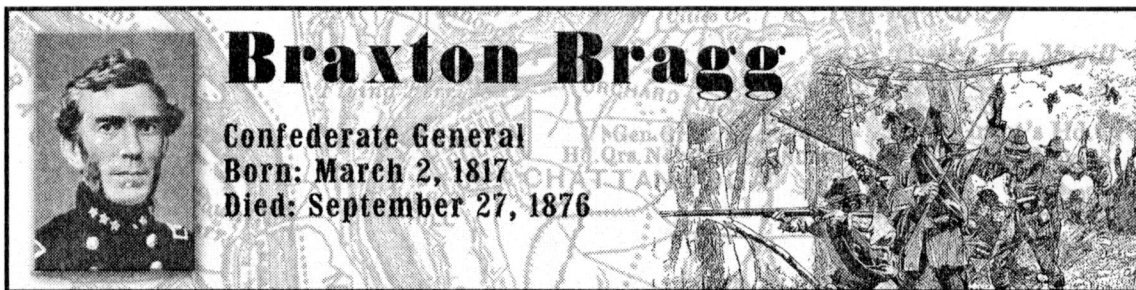

Braxton Bragg

Confederate General
Born: March 2, 1817
Died: September 27, 1876

One of the war's most controversial generals, Braxton Bragg, was born in Warrenton, North Carolina, in 1817. The son of a carpenter, Bragg was one of six siblings. The Braggs apparently struggled to find acceptance in upper southern society. Braxton's father sent him to a boys school in preparation for a military career at the age of 10.

Braxton's great memory skills helped him graduate 5th out of 50 cadets in West Point's class of 1837. He served as an artillery officer in the Seminole Wars and the Mexican-American War. Bragg forged a friendship during the Mexican-American War that had great implications for the Civil War. During the Battle of Buena Vista, Bragg arrived with his artillery unit to help Jefferson Davis' Mississippi regiment at a critical moment. Davis would repay the deed with lifelong loyalty.

Bragg was living on his Louisiana plantation when the war began. He was charged with the organization of defenses between Mobile and

General Rosecrans (LEFT) sits on a horse while Union artillery fires at advancing Rebel troops during the Battle of Stones River.

Braxton Bragg poses in his Confederate officer's uniform.

Pensacola. In the war's early days, he earned a reputation as a good troop trainer who could efficiently organize and supply an army.

Though blessed with great military knowledge, his indecisiveness, lack of people skills, and an inability to judge people would contribute to the Confederate State's defeat in the Western Theater. He proved ill-suited as a field commander. His failure to inspire confidence in his commanders led them to openly criticize him. His sharp manner and stern discipline resulted in his enlisted men viewing him as a tyrant. Some historians believe his problems can only be explained by health issues and his use of questionable medicines, including toxic mercury, that led to mental instability.

SHILOH TO STONES RIVER

Bragg commanded the Rebel right wing at Shiloh. Soon after the battle, Davis chose him to replace the ill P.G.T. Beauregard as commander of the Army of Tennessee (AoT). Charged with the near impossible job of defending Tennessee from a determined Union army, Bragg would lead the AoT through the struggles at Perryville, Stones River, Tullahoma, Chickamauga, and Chattanooga.

The Battle of Perryville was technically a southern victory. However, Bragg retreated soon after the battle, leaving behind more than 900 wounded men—and the state of Kentucky—in Union hands. The move greatly angered his generals who asked Davis to replace him.

Casualties at the Battle of Stones River from December 31, 1862 to January 2, 1863 amounted to more than one-third of the total forces involved on both sides. The southern generals blamed their heavy losses on Bragg. General Benjamin F. Cheatham vowed never to serve under him again after Bragg accused him of drunkenness. Former U.S. Vice President and Kentuckian John C. Breckinridge was outraged over Bragg's treatment of his men including the execution of a man whom he felt was innocent.

Benjamin Franklin Cheatham

CHICKAMAUGA

In early September 1863, General William Rosecrans began a drive on Chattanooga. Bragg gave up Chattanooga rather than risk having his supply line to Atlanta cut. The ensuing Tullahoma Campaign resulted in the AoT being driven out of Tennessee. Southerners began to say that Bragg always retreated whether he won or lost.

Confederate troops pin Union forces against a bluff during the Battle of Chickamauga.

Bragg hoped to fight the Union in northern Georgia where mountain forests would favor his smaller army. The two sides maneuvered in the remote region for 10 days before the Battle of Chickamauga began. During this time, Bragg ordered several attacks, but his subordinates, who thoroughly distrusted him, failed to act on his orders.

On September 19, 1863, Bragg engaged Union forces under generals Thomas Crittenden and George Thomas near Chickamauga Creek. Most of the fighting took place in thick woods between small groups. Thomas was able to hold his position at great cost to both sides. General James Longstreet's reinforcements began to arrive late in the day, and Bragg planned to renew attack the next day.

The second day, Bragg sent Leonidas Polk's troops against Thomas on the Rebel right. The attack started late and made no progress. Bragg ordered Longstreet to strike along the left. A communications breakdown led Rosecrans to move troops to fill a nonexistent gap, creating a real gap right where Longstreet was concentrating his forces. Longstreet easily overran Rosecrans' headquarters, sending two Union corps in a panicked retreat back to Chattanooga. By noon, Thomas' corps was the only organized Union corps on the battlefield.

Rosecrans sent his chief of staff and future U.S. President James A. Garfield back to the battlefield with orders for Thomas to retreat. Outnumbered by Bragg and Longstreet, Thomas' troops maintained order and consolidated a defense. General Gordon Granger disobeyed orders and went to Thomas' aid. Thomas and Granger withdrew to Chattanooga after dark.

Bragg's officers were angry that he failed to pursue. Cavalry General Nathan Bedford Forrest went so far as to call Bragg a scoundrel and coward and asked, "What does he fight battles for?" Bragg was shaken by heavy losses including 10 generals and half of his artillery horses.

Though Chickamauga is considered one of the great Confederate victories of the war, it did little to improve the South's position. It only temporarily stalled the Union drive against Atlanta. Bragg settled for laying siege to Chattanooga, the city that he had given up without a fight weeks before.

Chickamauga was the bloodiest battle of the Western Theater with over 34,000 of the men engaged killed or wounded. The battle cemented the reputation of Thomas, who was thereafter known as the Rock of Chickamauga. The battle finished Rosecrans whom Lincoln described as "...confused and stunned like a duck hit on the head." U.S. Grant, the new head of the Department of the Mississippi, relieved Rosecrans and replaced him with Thomas.

CHATTANOOGA

The deteriorating state of the AoT's leadership led to a visit from Davis. In spite of protests by Longstreet, Forrest, and others, Davis ignored their pleas and kept Bragg in command at Chattanooga while transferring the most troublesome officers to other commands.

Lincoln went on record saying that capturing Chattanooga was as important as capturing Richmond. However, control of the city was tenuous after Chickamauga. Union soldiers were on half rations while horses were allowed to starve. Thomas' defiant claim, "I will hold the town till we starve" seemed likely to come true.

Union soldiers assault Missionary Ridge on November 23, 1865.

William T. Sherman and Joseph Hooker's armies moved rapidly via rail to open a path to Thomas. Organized by Secretary of War Edwin Stanton, the logistical feat was the furthest and fastest deployment of such a body of troops up to that time in history. Opening the "Cracker Line" allowed food and ammunition to finally reach the city in sufficient quantities.

By late November, Grant was ready to attack Bragg. On the 24th, Hooker and Sherman struck at Bragg's flanks. Hooker's men daringly scaled the fog-shrouded 1100-foot-high Lookout Mountain and drove the Rebels down the other side. Sherman's men captured the right flank of Missionary Ridge only to find that a large ravine separated it from the main ridge.

The next day, Patrick Cleburne's division repulsed Sherman's attack against the right flank of the Rebels on Missionary Ridge. Hooker's assault on the left was held up by a destroyed bridge and road obstacles. At mid-afternoon, Grant ordered Thomas to pin Bragg's men in the center and keep them from reinforcing the flanks.

Patrick Cleburne

Thomas' men remembered the pain of Chickamauga and felt that they had something to prove. Four divisions with over 20,000 men defied disaster by crossing an open expanse and quickly overwhelming the first trench line. The Rebels retreated up the steep hill followed by Thomas' men who were yelling "Chicka-mauga! Chickamauga!" Cleburne was able to delay the charge long enough for Bragg's army to retreat toward Atlanta. Though many reasons have been suggested for the unlikely victory, low morale due to Bragg's leadership was likely a major reason.

If defeat at Vicksburg and Gettysburg several months before had depressed Rebel spirits, then Chattanooga crushed almost all hope. Victory at Chattanooga paved the way for Sherman's invasion of Georgia and the March to the Sea that would devastate the heart of the Confederacy.

FLEEING WITH DAVIS

Bragg requested his own removal from command after Chickamauga and was replaced by Joseph E. Johnston. Davis brought Bragg to Richmond to serve as his military advisor. In the final days of the war, he assisted Davis in an attempt to escape. Bragg was captured with Davis on May 9, 1865.

His plantation was destroyed during the war, so he moved to Alabama where he worked as a civil engineer. He later moved to Galveston, Texas, where he died in 1876.

While Bragg had favorable military abilities, he did nothing to secure a positive legacy. His early success in Tennessee and Kentucky and victory at Chickamauga failed to salvage his reputation in the minds of Southerners. His inability to command and low standing with his men made him a convenient scapegoat for the Lost Cause.

George Henry Thomas

Union General
Born: July 31, 1816
Died: March 28, 1870

One of the North's greatest leaders was a true southerner. George Henry Thomas was the youngest son of a slave-owning family of planters in Virginia. As a teenager, he helped his widowed mother and sisters escape Nat Turner's slave rebellion.

Thomas performed well at West Point where he graduated 12th in his class. There he befriended many future Civil War leaders, including his roommate and future commander William T. Sherman. Thomas would spend his entire adult life serving in the U.S. Army. Tall and strongly built, he was an imposing figure

George Thomas posed for Civil War photographer Matthew Brady.

who was affectionately called "Pap Thomas" by his men.

Thomas's bravery at Monterrey and Buena Vista earned him promotions and the respect of fellow officers. In 1851, he began teaching cavalry and artillery at West Point. Many future Civil War leaders learned the craft of war under his instruction.

Thomas joined future Confederate leaders Albert S. Johnston and Robert E. Lee in Texas as part of the 2nd Cavalry Regiment in 1855. He served five years until suffering a face wound from an Indian arrow in 1860.

Believing his fighting days were over, Thomas was working to secure a teaching position at the Virginia Military Institute when the war began. The Governor of Virginia offered him a position as the head of the state's ordnance department, which he declined. Though he was loathe to fight against his native Virginia, Thomas felt bound by his oath to the Constitution. His sisters disowned him and never spoke to him again.

Thomas was given command of a Pennsylvania brigade at First Bull Run. His efforts soon after in the Shenandoah Valley earned him a promotion to command of a division in the Army of the Ohio (AotO).

In January 1862, Thomas led a force of 4000 to victory at Mill Springs over a similar-sized force. The small battle had large implications. It secured eastern Kentucky as one of the first Union victories in the Western Theater and gained Thomas national attention.

THE ROCK OF CHICKAMAUGA

Thomas proved determined and competent in the battles of Shiloh, Perryville, and Stones River. His fighting spirit was evident at Stones River where

HAL JESPERSEN

Horseshoe Ridge in Chickamauga & Chattanooga National Military Park is where George Thomas made the stand that earned him the nickname "Rock of Chickamauga."

he said, "This army can't retreat. Gentlemen, I know of no better place to die than right here."

His loyalty was displayed when he refused a promotion to replace his commander Don Carlos Buell in late 1862. He thought it would look like he targeted his job. William S. Rosecrans accepted the position instead. While the gesture showed humility, the upcoming Battle of Chickamauga would prove that the army would have been better off with Thomas in charge.

William S. Rosecrans

For all he had already accomplished, Chickamauga would be the defining event of Thomas' career. On the first day of battle, his troops maintained a defensive line against the brunt of the Confederate attack. On the second day, Rosecrans lost his nerve and fled while Thomas remained cool under fire. He organized broken units to cover the retreat and withdrew all troops in orderly fashion.

His actions made him a national hero and earned the undying respect of his men. Even Abraham Lincoln said, "It is doubtful whether his heroism and skill…has ever been surpassed in this world…" Thomas rightfully earned the nickname of the Rock of Chickamauga.

In mid-1864, Sherman's Army of the Cumberland was wreaking havoc in Georgia. Rebel leaders decided the best way to stop Sherman was to disrupt his long supply line winding back to Chattanooga and then through Tennessee to Nashville. Thomas was dispatched to lead the AotO to protect Tennessee.

General John Bell Hood, a former student of Thomas, led the 40,000-strong Army of the Tennessee (AotT) into Kentucky to recruit reinforcements. Hood and his army crossed the Tennessee River west of Chattanooga on October 31st. The AotO under Thomas and General John Schofield in Tennessee stood in the way. Thomas was with half of the army at Nashville while Schofield had the other half at Spring Hill.

John Schofield

Thomas ordered Schofield to bring his troops to Nashville. The combined force would outnumber Hood's. Hood knew that he must intercept Schofield, defeat him, and then turn against Thomas' remaining troops. The result of this strategy was the Battle of Franklin.

BATTLE OF FRANKLIN

Scholfield managed to slip past Hood. However, he was forced to stop at Franklin, a town 18 miles south of Nashville, because a lack of adequate bridges across the Harpeth River. Schofield's 30,000 men dug in, while engineers constructed new bridges.

Hood arrived several hours after Schofield on November 30th and ordered an immediate frontal assault against the unfinished Franklin defenses. Hood's generals argued against the attack to no avail. Historically, Hood has been unfairly accused of ordering the attack as punishment for lack of courage. In reality, there were no good options. The Franklin defenders would only strengthen their positions over time, and Thomas might arrive at any moment. Despite their misgivings, Hood's subordinates followed orders. Patrick

John Bell Hood

Cleburne, one of the most outspoken critics of the attack plan, said, "We will take the works or fall in the attempt."

The Battle of Franklin was unusual in that it was fought over a relatively small area, and it was one of the few night battles of the Civil War. Hood's attack did not begin until dusk around 4:00 pm. At that time, 22,000 Rebel troops—more numerous than the 15,000 sent on the infamous Pickett's Charge at Gettysburg—charged against the Union positions.

Emerson Opdyke

Without orders to do so, Union General Emerson Opdycke moved his troops from their reserve position to plug a gap and drive back Hood's men. Subsequent Rebel assaults conducted in the black of night failed to dislodge the bluecoats. Around 9:00 pm. the fight-

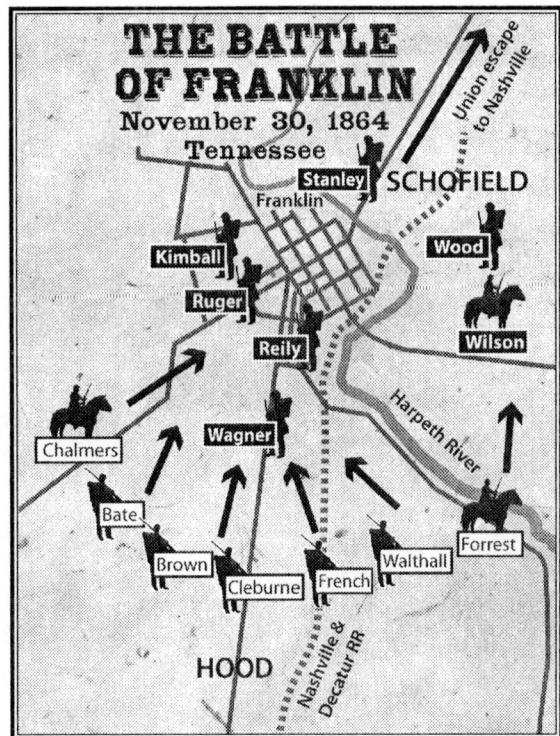

THE BATTLE OF FRANKLIN
November 30, 1864
Tennessee

Union escape to Nashville

SCHOFIELD
Stanley
Franklin
Kimball
Wood
Ruger
Reily
Wilson
Wagner
Chalmers
Bate
Brown
Cleburne
French
Walthall
Forrest
Harpeth River
Nashville & Decatur RR
HOOD

Elements of the Army of the Ohio cross the Harpeth River while John Bell Hood's men attack Union defenses during the Battle of Franklin.

ing dwindled into occasional artillery barrages, sniper fire, and scattered skirmishes. Around midnight, Schofield ordered his men across completed bridges to move to Nashville.

As morning broke on December 1st, the Rebels held the city of Franklin. Tragically, the victory was truly bittersweet. Hood lost 7000 men, three times the number of bluecoats. Six Confederate generals were killed, including Cleburne, and six others were wounded. Half of Hood's regimental commanders were killed or wounded. The Battle of Franklin has been called the "Gettysburg of the West" for both its impact and high casualty rate. Hood's AotT ceased to be a major force.

BATTLE OF NASHVILLE

Hood entrenched his remaining troops outside Nashville, but he had no definite plan other than to wait for reinforcements that would never arrive. Thomas ignored pleas from Secretary of War Edwin Stanton and U.S. Grant to make an immediate attack. Sherman had taken Thomas' best soldiers in Georgia. He needed the time to train new recruits and rest his fatigued veterans.

Two weeks after the Battle of Franklin, Thomas sent 50,000 soldiers against Hood's 25,000. Against all odds, Hood's men refused to fold in the day-long struggle but instead retreated and created a shorter line.

Union artillery and cavalry forces rout the Confederate Army during the Battle of Nashville.

Rebel resistance collapsed on the second day, and the AoT dissolved. Thousands of men surrendered while others threw down their weapons and fled from the field. Union cavalry hunted stragglers over the next two weeks. Nathan Bedford Forrest's cavalry delayed the pursuit at almost every creek and river.

Survivors trickled into Tupelo, Mississippi, in early January, but the AoT's strength was only half what it had been two months earlier. A sorrowful Hood resigned on January 13, 1865.

CONTINUING SERVICE

Congress recognized Thomas' role in defeating Hood. Thomas retained command of the AoTO for the remainder of the war and into Reconstruction. Impressed with the performance of African American troops under his command, the Virginian became a staunch supporter of freedmen's rights. He died of a stroke in 1870 shortly after transferring to the Army of the Pacific in San Francisco.

As the first high-profile Union general to die after the war, Thomas' death generated much interest. Crowds came out to view his coffin as it traveled east. President Grant and other high profile government officials attended his funeral. He was buried in New York near his wife's home because his native Virginia considered him a traitor.

For his consistency and contributions, Thomas ranks alongside Grant and Sherman as the Union's most successful Famous Men. He won an early victory at Mill Springs, made a glorious stand at Chickamauga, and brought the war in the Western Theater to a close.

William Tecumseh Sherman

**Union General
Born: February 8, 1820
Died: February 14, 1891**

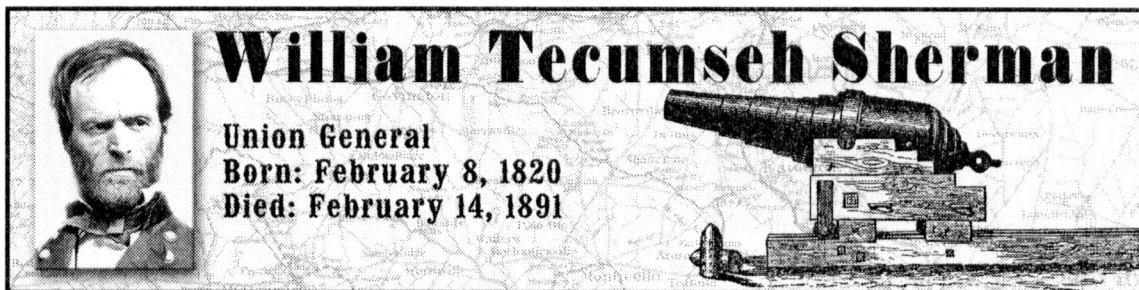

William Tecumseh Sherman once said, "War is cruelty. There is no use trying to reform it, the crueler it is, the sooner it will be over." Embracing this axiom, Sherman played a crucial role in leading the Union to victory.

Born in Lancaster, Ohio in 1820, Sherman lost his father at an early age. A family friend and future U.S. senator, Thomas Ewing, agreed to raise Sherman in order to relieve financial stress on his mother. Sherman's adoptive father helped him secure an appointment to West Point.

After graduation, William participated in the Seminole Wars and helped move Native Americans to Oklahoma over the Trail of Tears. A number of extended trips across the South on military business familiarized him with the terrain over which he would later march.

General Sherman surveys a battlefield.

While serving in California in 1848, he confirmed reports of the discovery of gold at Sutter's Mill and sent news to the eastern United States. His army pay could not keep up with rapid inflation caused by the ensuing gold rush, so he resigned. He showed his administrative skills by working as an executive in several businesses.

In the days leading up to secession, Sherman was serving as the superintendent of a seminary and military academy that would later become Louisiana State University. He left because he was passionate that the Union must be preserved at any cost and viewed secession as a mistake that would bring ruin upon the South.

NERVOUS BREAKDOWN

Shortly before First Bull Run, Sherman returned to the U.S. Army as a colonel. He proved his worth during Bull Run by leading his unit in an orderly retreat from field while protecting the rest of the Union army. The battle confirmed what Sherman had understood long before many others—the war would be long and costly.

After Bull Run, Sherman was promoted to brigadier general and placed over the Department of the Cumberland. His mental state declined as the gravity of the war weighed heavily upon him. After several complaints to Washington and angry outbursts directed at journalists, he returned home to rest in December 1861.

Sherman's sanity benefitted from the time off. Several months later he began supplying Ulysses S. Grant from Cairo, Illinois before joining him in the field. Thus began what was perhaps the greatest partnership of the war.

CONTRIBUTIONS IN THE WESTERN THEATER

In early April 1862, Sherman was headquartered near Shiloh Meeting House, a one-room log church in Tennessee. Sherman told Grant that he did not expect an attack. When the Rebels did attack on April 6th, Sherman rode forward to reconnoiter the situation. Sherman was hit on the hand by buckshot and cried, "My God, we're attacked!"

Sherman's 5th Division helped hold the right flank of the Union line on the first day of Shiloh long enough to buy time for Grant to organize defensive lines. After the initial shock, Sherman grew calmer as the day progressed.

Sherman began to develop the conviction that the South must intensely feel the war in order to surrender. In an October 4, 1862 letter to Grant, Sherman wrote, "We cannot change the hearts of the people of the South but we can make war so terrible that they will realize the fact that however brave and gallant and devoted to their country, still they are mortal and should exhaust all peaceful remedies before they fly to war."

On December 28, 1862, Grant ordered an attack at Chickasaw Bluffs, in one of the first attempts to reach Vicksburg, Mississippi. The assault was doomed from the start. Sherman's troops attacked well-protected Confederate positions on the bluffs. Men who successfully crossed the swamp in front of the positions found themselves pinned at the base of the bluffs. Many could not retreat until after nightfall. Sherman's men sustained 1200 casualties while the Rebels only suffered 187.

LIBRARY OF CONGRESS

A fanciful view of Sherman's March to the Sea includes the burning of barns, destruction of railroads, and masses of refugees.

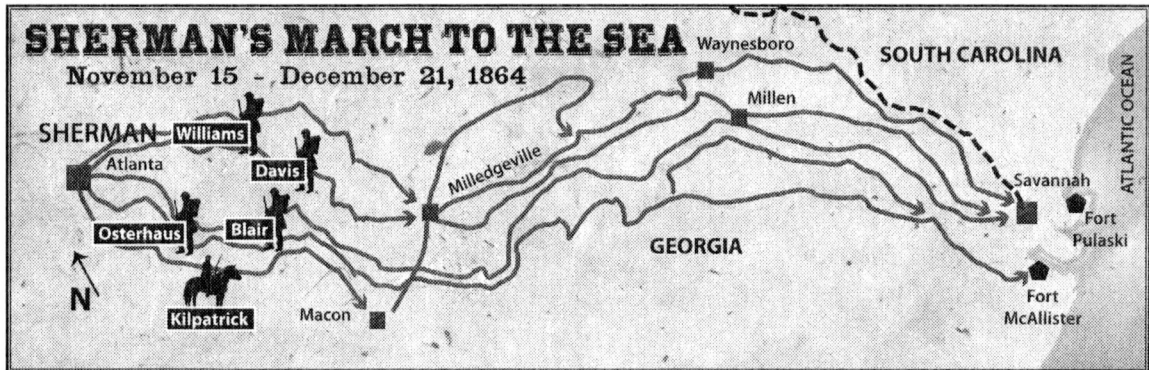

THE MARCH TO THE SEA

Subsequent questionable attacks against the Vicksburg defenses led Sherman to dislike frontal assaults, saying, "Its glory is all moonshine; even success the most brilliant is over dead and mangled bodies, with the anguish and lament of distant families."

After Union success at Chattanooga, Sherman and Grant plotted the course to end the war. Sherman would go after Joseph E. Johnston while Grant would destroy Lee. During the Atlanta Campaign in 1864, Sherman avoided direct assaults and instead used his superior numbers to flank Johnston's lines and force him to retreat. In this way, Sherman's troops advanced to Atlanta with relatively few casualties.

Sherman besieged Atlanta and set about cutting off supply routes. Confederate General John Bell Hood was compelled to abandon Atlanta on September 1st, but not until after setting ammunition stores on fire and driving out most of its citizens.

Sherman's enduring legacy is his march through Georgia that cut the Confederacy in two. The goal was not victory in battle as Sherman explained, "The simple fact that a man's home has been visited by an enemy makes a soldier very, very anxious to get home to look after his family and property."

After announcing to all that he was marching from Atlanta to the sea, Sherman then broke communications. The march by 55,000 men and 7000 cavalry began in November 1864. Union leaders and citizens waited with great anticipation to hear word about his success or failure. Citizens in Georgia waited with a feeling of dread.

The weather cooperated, and Rebel resistance was light. Sherman's troops stripped the land of food, confiscated livestock, and burned barns and other means of production while taking care not to harm civilians.

The relatively few atrocities were committed by stragglers who were only marginally part of the army. Many blacks, now freedmen, followed Sherman even though he refused to take charge of their care. Rumors of Union aggres-

General Sherman poses with his staff.

Workers survey the damage to a railroad roundhouse after the Battle of Atlanta.

siveness—some slaves were told Union soldiers threw blacks into fires—proved unfounded. Some Union soldiers cared for and adopted orphans along the way.

Morale was high in Sherman's army, knowing that they crippling the Confederacy while enjoying the zest of living off the land. With the capture of Fort McAllister on December 13th, Sherman had reached the sea. Receiving reinforcement by sea, Sherman soon captured Savannah, Georgia, and telegraphed President Lincoln, "I beg to present you as a Christmas gift the City of Savannah, with one hundred and fifty guns and plenty of ammunition, also about twenty-five thousand bales of cotton."

CAROLINA CAMPAIGN

Sherman marched north with the expectation of linking up with Grant's army in Virginia. This required cutting through South Carolina, the birthplace of secession. The March to the Sea had taken place during a dry fall and involved crossing few rivers. The Carolina Campaign required the crossing of nine major rivers during a wet winter. Soldiers and contraband freedmen literally cut their way through the forests, using the logs to build corduroy roads through the Salkehatchie Swamp.

Columbia, South Carolina, fell to Sherman's army on February 17, 1865. By midnight, the entire city was bathed in the glow of

Flames spread quickly over Columbia, South Carolina on the night of February 17-18, 1865.

The Columbia, South Carolina fire utterly decimated the city.

bright orange flames. The origin of the fire has been debated over the years. It was probably a combination of burning cotton left behind by Rebels, former slaves and released prisoners reveling in their freedom, and drunken Union soldiers. Southerners were convinced that Sherman was directly responsible. Sherman later said of the burning of Columbia, "Though I never ordered it and never wished it, I have never shed many tears over the event, because I believe it hastened what we all fought for, the end of the war."

Sherman pursued Joseph E. Johnston's army into North Carolina. His final significant battle was a victory over Johnston at the Battle of Bentonville in March 1865. Grant and Lincoln met with Sherman on a boat at City Point on the James River to plan the final

General Sherman's troops cross the Edisto River in South Carolina.

days of the war. Sherman accepted Johnston's surrender in April, effectively ending the war in the Eastern Theater. His desire to reestablish rights to southern citizens under the Constitution was rebuffed by Secretary of War Edwin Stanton, and Johnston was eventually offered the same terms that Grant extended to Lee at Appomattox.

GENERAL OF THE ARMY

The destroyer of railroads during the war, Sherman was given the ironic task of protecting the construction of the transcontinental railroad. Though sympathetic towards Native Americans, he told them, "You cannot stop the locomotives any more than you can stop the sun or moon."

In 1869, Sherman succeeded Grant as General of the Army, a post he held for 14 years. During visits to the South, he was received with respect with the noted exception of South Carolina. In 1871, he went on a foreign tour visiting Europe, North Africa, Russia, and Turkey.

Popular support began to swell for Sherman to run for President in the 1884 election. Sherman would have nothing to do with it, stating, "I will not accept if nominated and will not serve if elected."

Pneumonia, complicated by lifelong asthma, was Sherman's cause of death on February 14, 1891. Sherman was buried in St. Louis. Thousands of former soldiers turned out to pay their final respects. Also attending was Sherman's adversary, 84-year-old Joseph Johnston. The funeral, held on a cold, rainy day, made Johnston ill. He died one month later also of pneumonia.

The preservation of the Union can be significantly attributed to Sherman's leadership and his partnership with Grant. Sherman's tactics in taking the fight from the battlefield directly to the enemy homeland were revolutionary and have influenced every major war since. Therefore, historians regard Sherman as the first "modern" general, and we acknowledge his prominence among the Famous Men.

Musician Alphonzo Smith composed a special march in honor of William Sherman after his death.

Nathan Bedford Forrest

Confederate Cavalry General
Born: July 13, 1821
Died: October 29, 1877

Many of the South's Famous Men were born into privileged families and received extensive military training before the Civil War began. This was not the case for Nathan Bedford Forrest. Born in Chapel Hill, Tennessee, and raised by a blacksmith, Forrest received less than six months of schooling. While still 16, he took responsibility for his family after his father died. Forrest proved to be a gifted businessman as he became a millionaire dealing in the South's three great commodities: land, cotton, and slaves.

A Natural Leader

When the Civil War began, Forrest volunteered as a private. He soon decided to raise a unit of his own at his expense. His call to recruit was blunt and revealed why he would become revered in the South and hated by Northerners: "I wish none but those who desire to be actively engaged. Come on boys, if you want a heap of fun and to kill some Yankees."

Though he had no military training, Forrest proved to be a decisive, natural leader. Forrest and his men were at Fort Donelson when General Buckner agreed to surrender to Ulysses S. Grant. Refusing to give up, Forrest led 1500 cavalry and infantry to slip away without a shot. He fought Grant again at Shiloh, where Forrest's cavalry covered the Confederate retreat.

Forrest's promotion to brigadier general in the Army of the Tennessee led to heated disputes with Braxton Bragg, Joe Wheeler, and others. It was clear that Forrest would best serve the South in an independent command. In the summer of 1862, he began a series of lightning raids that earned him the nickname "The Wizard of the Saddle." In one raid on Murfreesboro,

Braxton Bragg

Tennessee, he captured 1000 Union prisoners in addition to weapons and supplies. After a string of victories, he said that he had "put the skeer on 'em," regarding Union soldiers.

Rebel infantry highly respected Forrest. This was a testimony to his leadership, aggressiveness, and willingness to fight in the thickest parts of battle, as infantry typically detested cavalry. Bedford was injured four times and had nearly thirty horses shot out or injured from under him. A staff officer under Union General James Wilson meeting Bedford during a truce observed, "To think quickly and concretely, and to decide likewise, seem to be his mental habit. There was about his talk and manner a certain soldierly simplicity and engaging frankness and I was frequently lost in real admiration."

In September 1863, Forrest commanded a corps under Bragg during the Battle of Chickamauga. Livid at Bragg for not immediately pursuing Union troops after the victory, Forrest said, "You have played the part of a...scoundrel, and are a coward, and if you were any part of a man I would slap your jaws and force you to resent it."

TRIVIA

General Joe Wheeler served as a general in the Confederate Army and later in the U.S. Army during the Spanish-American war.

Today, Fort Pillow is on the grounds of Fort Pillow State Park in western Tennessee.

Bedford reached the conclusion before most southern leaders that the war was unwinnable, saying, "Any man who is in favor of a further prosecution of this war is a fit subject for a lunatic asylum, and ought to be sent there immediately." His opinion did not prevent him from continuing to fight.

In April 1864, Forrest was at the center of one of the darkest moments of the war—the Fort Pillow Massacre. Forrest's soldiers easily captured Fort Pillow on the Mississippi River near Memphis, Tennessee, but killed 262 soldiers of the 6th U.S. Colored Heavy Artillery in doing so.

Northern investigators concluded that the killings were done in cold blood. Southerners claimed that the defenders refused to give up and fought to the death. Forrest admitted that unarmed blacks were killed, but it was not clear whether the murders were ordered by Forrest or other officers, or if they were initiated by disobedient soldiers. For the rest of the war, African-American soldiers used "Remember Fort Pillow" as a battle cry.

Forrest caused enough trouble behind Sherman's lines during the Atlanta campaign that Sherman said, "That devil Forrest...must be hunted down and killed if it costs ten thousand lives and bankrupts the Federal treasury." In the summer of 1864, Sherman sent Union General Samuel Sturgis to eliminate Forrest's threat to destroy a Nashville and Chattanooga Railroad line supplying Sherman's troops.

THE BATTLE OF BRICE'S CROSSROADS

Forrest's regiment defeated Sturgis's troops at Brice's Crossroads. This minor battle serves as a prime example of Forrest's ability to lead men and use tactical skill to defeat larger opponents.

Sturgis's Union column boasted 4800 infantry, 3300 cavalry, and 400 artillerymen with 22 guns. The troops boasted combat experience and many of the cavalrymen were armed with the newest Colt repeating rifles. In contrast, Forrest only had about 2000 cavalry, 1500 infantry, and two artillery batteries of four guns each.

Samuel Sturgis

Several skirmishes between patrols occurred in the days leading up to the battle. Forrest assumed a position at Brice's Crossroads on a hill overlooking a bridge crossing the Tishomingo Creek. He knew that the Union would have to cross the creek at that point. The battle took place on a hot June day. The Union cavalry arrived first, crossed the bridge, and engaged Forrest's troops east of the Crossroads. Forrest knew that the Union cavalry was unsupported and vulnerable as it was three hours ahead of the Union infantry.

A vigorous attack drove the Union back to the crossroads and down towards Tishomingo Creek. Forrest's cavalry enveloped the Union flanks, and artillery fired grapeshot, sending the cavalry into retreat. Confederate artillery had a clear shot across the creek as Union soldiers and horses recrossed and fled up the opposite hill. Pursuing the fleeing cavalry, Forrest's men rudely met the late-arriving Union infantry

AUTHOR PHOTO

This footbridge at Brice's Crossroads National Battlefield Site sits on the same spot as the bridge where Forrest's men clashed with Union cavalry.

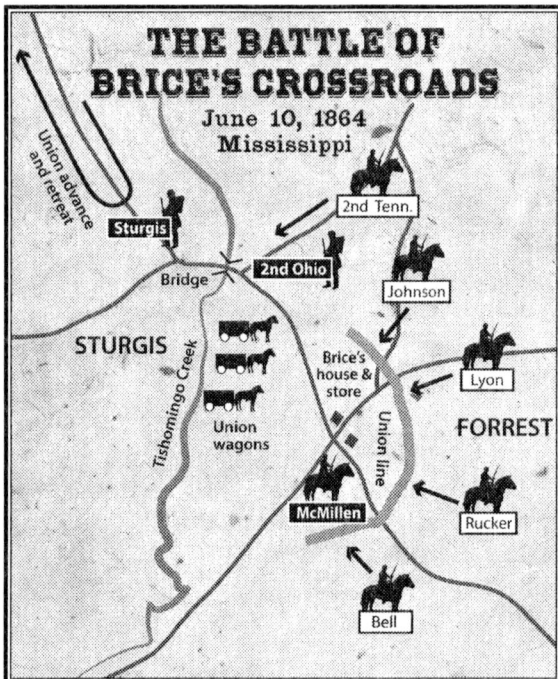

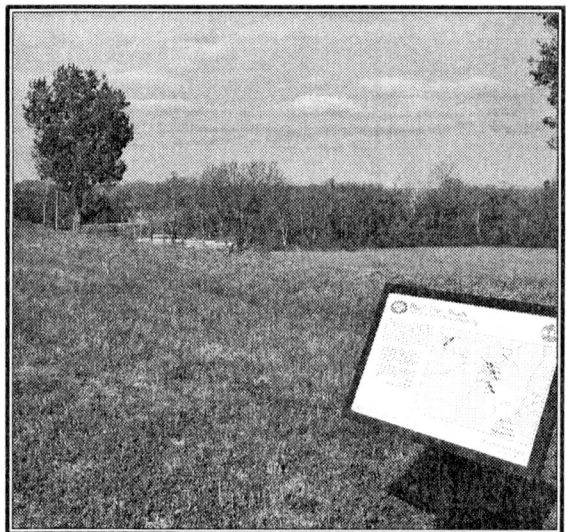

AUTHOR PHOTO

A marker at Brice's Crossroads National Battlefield Site in northern Mississippi stands on the hill overlooking the bridge at Tishomingo Creek.

Forrest's 1864 raid on Memphis stirred much anxiety in northerners, but failed in its primary objective of freeing Confederate prisoners from Irving Block Prison.

by pushing them back over several ridges and streams. The Rebels and unrelenting weather were too much for the fatigued and underfed Union soldiers.

Forrest captured 16 cannons, many small weapons, ammunition, and dozens of wagons filled with Union supplies. Federal casualties were grave, including 223 killed, 394 wounded, and 1623 missing. An additional 1600 were captured. In contrast, just 96 Confederate soldiers died, and 396 suffered wounds.

Unlike many Civil War leaders who failed to press an advantage, Forrest pursued and harassed the fleeing column for 55 miles. He gave credit to his artillery for moving up quickly and engaging the enemy at close range. The stinging defeat led Sturgis to resign his command.

FIRST DEFEAT AND POST-WAR CONTROVERSY

Forrest's first defeat took place in early 1865 at the Battle of Tupelo. General Wilson led a raid south from Tennessee toward Selma, Ala-bama. Learning that Forrest was near, Wilson entrenched near Tupelo and awaited Forrest's attack. The ill-advised attack under the intense July sun failed to move the entrenched men, and Forrest retreated. Sherman was upset that Wilson did not pursue. However, Forrest's effectiveness was irreversibly diminished after this battle. Forrest continued to make minor raids until the end of the war and did not give up until May 9, 1865, a month after Robert E. Lee's surrender at Appomattox.

The war was costly for Forrest as he lost his slaves, plantation, and fortune. He used his natural business skills to start over and began farming. He later served as a railroad president during which time he founded a store in a town that became Forrest City, Arkansas. Ruined by the financial panic of 1873, Forrest lived out his final days in a cabin with his wife while operating a prison work camp on President's Island in the Mississippi River. He died of diabetes in Memphis on October 29, 1877.

Nathan Bedford Forrest remains one of the most polarizing leaders from the war period. After the war, he joined the Ku Klux Klan and reportedly served as the organization's first Grand Dragon. Some accounts claim that he worked to break up the organization in 1869, though this was supposedly to gain support from Republicans for his new railroad venture and not out of conscience.

Whatever moral shortcomings Forrest might have had, his leadership skills were unquestionable. He was one of just a few men to enlist as private and later become an officer. Both Lee and Jefferson Davis lamented that they had not taken full advantage of Forrest's skills. Forrest is buried in a city park in Memphis, Tennessee.

Robert Edward Lee

Confederate General
Born: January 19, 1807
Died: October 12, 1870

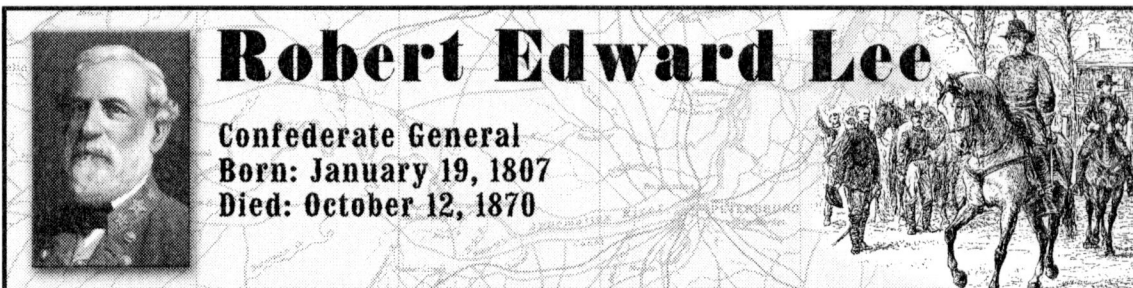

The iconic leader of the Lost Cause, Robert E. Lee was revered by Southerners and grudgingly respected by Northerners. Lee was the son of a Revolutionary War hero and head of one of Virginia's leading families, Henry "Light-Horse Harry" Lee III. The Virginia ties were strengthened when Robert married a descendant of George Washington's adopted son.

LIBRARY OF CONGRESS

General Robert E. Lee poses in his Confederate general's uniform for photographer Julian Vannerson.

A DISTINGUISHED CAREER

Robert graduated second to Charles Mason in the West Point class of 1829. Mason only served in the military for two years before leaving to pursue business ventures. In contrast, Lee devoted over 30 years to the U.S. Army.

Lee's first assignment was engineering coastal defenses and harbors. He served on General Winfield Scott's staff during the Mexican-American War, earning the respect of his commander by showing bravery, initiative, and leadership skills on multiple occasions. Scott considered Lee the Union's best officer and the "best soldier I ever saw in the field." During the war, Lee

Winfield Scott

became familiar with many of the men he would serve with—or against—during the Civil War.

The 1850s were an interesting decade for Lee. In 1852, he was named superintendent of West Point. In 1855, he joined the legendary 2nd Cavalry in Texas under Albert S. Johnston. In 1859, he led U.S. marines in putting down the John Brown raid. When the Civil War began, he was in charge of the Department of Texas.

Lee turned down an offer to lead the Union Army, thus creating a great "What if?" of the war. The offer was made on April 18, 1861, the same day that Lee learned of Virginia's secession. Lee was against secession right up until Virginia joined the Confederacy. Once the decision was made, he said, "I cannot raise my hand against my birthplace, my home, my children." He was

General Lee sits astride his horse, Traveller.

appointed commander-in-chief of Virginia's forces five days later.

Lee understood the challenges faced by the South. He said, "I foresee that the country will have to pass through a terrible ordeal, a necessary expiation perhaps for our national sins." His attempt to secure western Virginia from Union troops was frustrated when he lost his first battle at Cheat Mountain, Virginia, (now a part of West Virginia) on September 11, 1861.

After Johnston was injured at Seven Pines during the Peninsula campaign, Lee was given charge of the Army of Northern Virginia (AoNV). Though his exploits as commander of the AoNV have taken on a legendary quality, his appointment was not popular in southern papers at the time. The *Richmond Examiner* insulted him with a sarcastic nickname, "Evacuating Lee, who has never yet risked a single battle with the invader."

Lee's Northern Virginia Campaign was the natural response to Union General George McClellan's failed Peninsula Campaign. Some scholars consider this to be Lee's most brilliant campaign. Sensing that the North was demoralized and vulnerable, his trusted generals Jonathan Thomas "Stonewall" Jackson and James Long-street invaded the North in September 1862. Despite McClellan's bumbling and indecisiveness, Lee's effort faltered at Antietam.

HIGH WATER MARK
OF THE CONFEDERACY

Victories at Fredericksburg in late 1862 and Chancellorsville in May 1863 inspired Lee to plan another invasion. Lee convinced Jefferson Davis that an invasion of Pennsylvania could turn the tide of the war. The decision negatively affected the Confederacy in two ways. First, the AoNV's capability to take to the offensive was effectively ended after defeat at Gettysburg. Second, reinforcements destined for Vicksburg were instead sent to Lee. Vicksburg would fall just one day after Gettysburg in July.

At Gettysburg, Lee took blame for the failure of Pickett's Charge which actually involved two other divisions besides Pickett's. He rode among his men saying "It's all my fault, it is I who have lost this fight." One month later, he offered his resignation to Davis, saying, "No one is more aware than myself of inability for the duties of my position. I cannot even accomplish what I myself desire. How can I fulfill the expectations of others?" Davis refused to accept the resignation.

THE WILDERNESS

In March 1864, Ulysses S. Grant was given command of all U.S. armies. In May he attached his headquarters to George Meade's Army of the Potomac (AotP). Breaking winter camp, Grant and the AotP began the Virginia Overland Campaign to battle Lee.

Gouvenour K. Warren

The Battle of the Wilderness fought over May 5-7, 1864, was the first meeting between Grant and Lee. Meade sent General Gouverneur Warren's V Corps through a thick wood-

The Battle of the Wilderness was a desperate struggle in a wooded area of rural Virginia.

ed area known as the Wilderness. It was the same area where Lee had defeated Joseph Hooker a year before. During the back-and-forth fighting, Lee had a horse shot from under him.

Grant lost 20,000 men, twice as many as Lee. However, he was different from other Union commanders and continued to press Lee. Grant pulled his army and attempted to place it between Lee and Richmond. Lee responded by blocking Grant at Spotsylvania Court House.

SPOTSYLVANIA COURT HOUSE

Lee sent a corps under Richard Anderson to block Meade's advance at a crossroads at Spotsylvania on May 8th. Grant's attack on the 10th was repulsed, but he refused to let up the pressure. Another attack on May 12th raged into the night.

It centered on a bend in the lines that became known as the Bloody Angle. Neither side gained an advantage, and both sides eventually settled near their original lines.

Several minor skirmishes took place over the next five days. On the 19th, Lee launched a failed assault against the strong Union defenses.

TRIVIA

At Spotsylvania, aides cautioned Union General John Sedgewick near front lines. He said, "They couldn't hit an elephant at this distance," moments before a sharpshooter hit him below the left eye, killing him instantly.

While the Rebels regrouped, Grant shifted his armies to the southeast. This forced Lee to move once again between the AotP and Richmond. The Union suffered 18,000 casualties at Spotsylvania Court House, while the Rebels suffered 9000.

COLD HARBOR

Grant ordered Philip Sheridan's cavalry to capture Cold Harbor, a hotel that did not serve meals, situated 10 miles northeast of Richmond. Sheridan's cavalry, armed with superior Colt repeating rifles, met Confederate cavalry under Fitzhugh Lee and pushed them back.

After consolidating his forces, Grant ordered repeated attacks on June 3rd that even his own men regarded as futile. One soldier despairingly wrote in his diary, "June 3, 1864, Cold Harbor. I was killed."

Over the next nine days, the two sides traded artillery and sniper fire but made no direct attacks. On the 13th, Grant moved east toward the rail center of Petersburg in another effort to cut off Richmond. Lee reacted quickly, beating Grant to Petersburg.

Northern newspapers called Grant a butcher, accusing him of wasting human lives at Cold Harbor. Grant later confessed that he regretted pressing the attacks. Cold Harbor was Lee's last victory, and it succeeded in buying the South another 10 months.

LIBRARY OF CONGRESS

The Battle of Spotsylvania Court House as painted by Thure de Thulstrup.

The Burnett Inn in Hanover County, Virginia was the cold harbor (hotel without hot meals) that inspired the name of one of the bloodiest battles of the Civil War.

PETERSBURG CAMPAIGN

Petersburg, Virginia, was the seventh-largest city in the Confederacy. When Lee's army arrived, it occupied and reinforced trenches dug by P.G.T. Beauregard's men. On June 18th, 850 men of the 1st Maine Heavy Artillery advanced upon the stout Rebel defenses. Within 10 minutes, 632 Maine men were killed or wounded. This one tragic example established the Petersburg Campaign as the prototype for the trench warfare of the First World War.

Grant's severing of rail and road connections involved a series of smaller battles and skirmishes. He launched nine distinctive attacks during the campaign, using his superior numbers to simultaneously attack north and south of the James River. Grant's third assault, launched in July 1864, resulted in the ill-fated Battle of the Crater.

On March 25, 1865, Lee launched an attack to the east against Fort Stedman in hopes of drawing off Union troops. The attack failed, weakening Lee's position in the process. This set up the Battle of Five Forks and the subsequent breaking of Confederate lines.

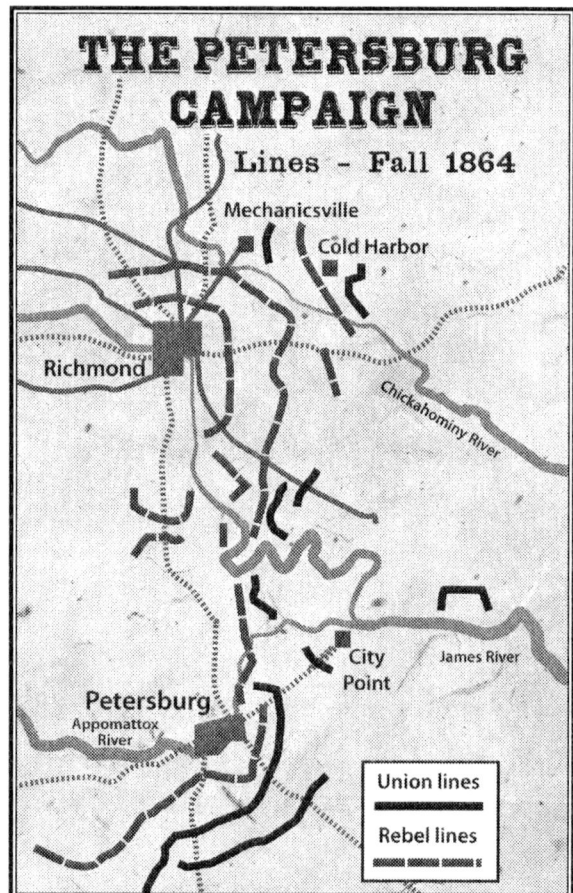

THE PETERSBURG CAMPAIGN

Lines - Fall 1864

Mechanicsville
Cold Harbor
Richmond
Chickahominy River
City Point
James River
Petersburg
Appomattox River

Union lines
Rebel lines

Grant sent Sheridan's cavalry to capture an important rail junction called Five Forks on April 1st. Lee had entrusted George Pickett to hold Five Forks at all costs. Once again, Pickett would go down on the wrong side of history. He and fellow officers were enjoying a shad (fish) bake two miles away while the battle occurred. Sheridan turned the Rebel flanks and captured many prisoners.

With his final supply route cut off, Lee notified Jefferson Davis to evacuate Richmond. Lee abandoned Petersburg after dark on April 2nd with the goal of linking up with Joseph E. Johnston's army. The human toll of the Petersburg Campaign was 42,000 Union and 28,000 Rebel casualties.

The McLean House where General Lee surrendered the Army of Northern Virginia to General Grant.

SURRENDER AT APPOMATTOX

After a brief battle on April 8th, Union forces surrounded Lee's army at the village of Appomattox Court House. Rather than see his army destroyed, Lee lamented, "...there is nothing left me but to go and see General Grant." Grant offered Lee and his fellow officers generous terms, allowing them to be paroled rather than taken prisoner. Grant even allowed Lee to keep his horse and sword.

Despite defeat, Lee was, and remains, a revered southern hero. After the war, he became president of Washington University. He served there until heart disease claimed his life in 1870. In 1975, Congress posthumously restored Lee's U.S. citizenship.

Lee's leadership as a fierce soldier contrasts with his enduring image as a quiet gentleman. Lee's strengths included his determination and devotion to duty and intimate knowledge of the generals he fought. His ambitions fell short when on the offensive, but he excelled in testing the resolve of the North when fighting a defensive war.

Raphael Semmes

Confederate Naval Captain
Born: September 27, 1809
Died: August 30, 1877

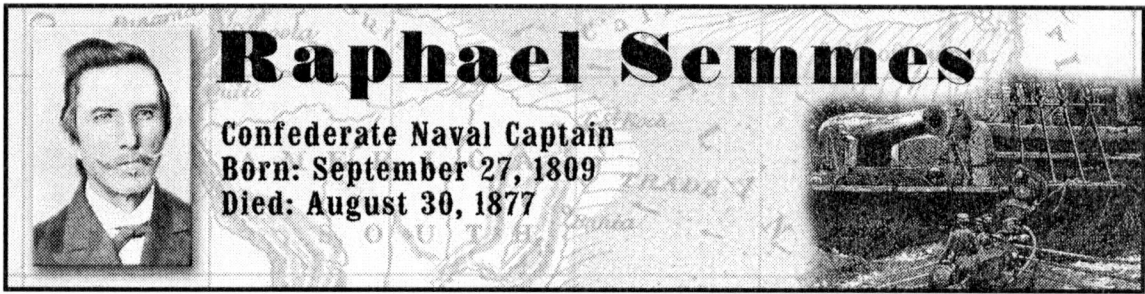

Confederate naval hero Raphael Semmes was born on his family's tobacco farm in Maryland. Both of his parents died before he was 15. Semmes went to live with his uncle Benedict "Ben" Semmes, a doctor and politician, who encouraged the habit of reading. Raphael later said, "The habit of study is in itself a great comfort." Time spent with two other uncles who were merchant ship captains sparked a love for sailing. Uncle Ben helped Raphael secure an appointment as a midshipman in the U.S. Navy.

People who met Raphael during and after the war expected a fiery naval hero but were surprised to meet an unassuming man who was slight of build. Semmes spent 35 years in the U.S. Navy but advanced slowly because of frequent clashes with superiors and a glut of officers during peacetime. In his civilian life, he worked as a lawyer in Mobile, Alabama, while raising his five children with his Northern wife.

During the Mexican-American War, Lieutenant Semmes shared a cabin with Lieutenant John Winslow. The two men would later command opposing ships in a fateful battle. Semmes had a brief command as captain of the USS *Somers*, a 10-gun ship with two masts. The ship capsized during a storm. Semmes' memoirs of his time during the war gained him national recognition.

Promotion to commander in 1855 only gained Semmes a short stint commanding the mail steamer *Illinois*. He then oversaw lighthouses until 1860.

A PATCHWORK NAVY

At the start of the Civil War, the United States only had 42 commissioned warships. The leader of the U.S. Navy was Gideon Welles, whom Abraham Lincoln called Father Neptune. Welles organized northern merchant marines ships in an effort to enforce Winfield Scott's Anaconda Plan to blockade southern ports.

The Confederate States had no navy and only a single shipyard at Norfolk when the war began. There were no facilities capable of building engines large enough for sea worthy ships.

Secretary of the Navy Stephen R. Mallory attempted to overcome these shortcomings by press-

THE PHOTOGRAPHIC HISTORY OF THE CIVIL WAR

Raphael Semmes poses in civilian clothes.

Gideon Welles

ing commercial ships into use as a coastal fleet. They mined the entrances to harbors and rivers rather than engage more powerful Union warships. Small torpedo boats approached and mounted mines on Union ships with the use of long spars. Mallory's most memorable rebuilding project was to convert the *Merrimack* into the ironclad CSS *Virginia*.

Semmes commanded a light, five-gun ship, the CSS *Sumter*. After breaking the Union blockade and raiding in the Caribbean, Semmes started across the Atlantic. The old boat survived a three-day storm but had to be abandoned at Gibraltar because it was beyond repair. Semmes bided his time waiting for a new command.

CSS ALABAMA

James D. Bulloch was the top Confederate foreign agent in Great Britain. He oversaw the secret construction of a three-mast, coal-powered ship designed for speed and extended cruis-

ing. The ship left Liverpool unarmed and with a light crew. It rendezvoused with Semmes and a coaling ship, the *Agrippina*, at the Azores off the coast of Portugal. After outfitting eight cannons, including a pivoting Blakely rifle firing 7-inch, 100-pound shells, the ship began a legendary cruise in August 1862 as the raider CSS *Alabama*.

The *Alabama's* first prize, the *Ocmulgee*, was a whaling ship out of Massachusetts. All the sailors were taken prisoner, and the whaler burned to the waterline. The *Alabama* captured nine more ships in the Eastern Atlantic before heading to the Newfoundland Grand Banks to target Yankee ships carrying grain to Europe. As news about the *Alabama* filtered back to the United States, one newspaper labeled Semmes "a Pirate on the High Seas."

In late 1862, the *Alabama* moved into the Gulf of Mexico. The next month, she surprised and sank the USS *Hatteras* near Galveston in her first military engagement. In mid-1863, the *Alabama*

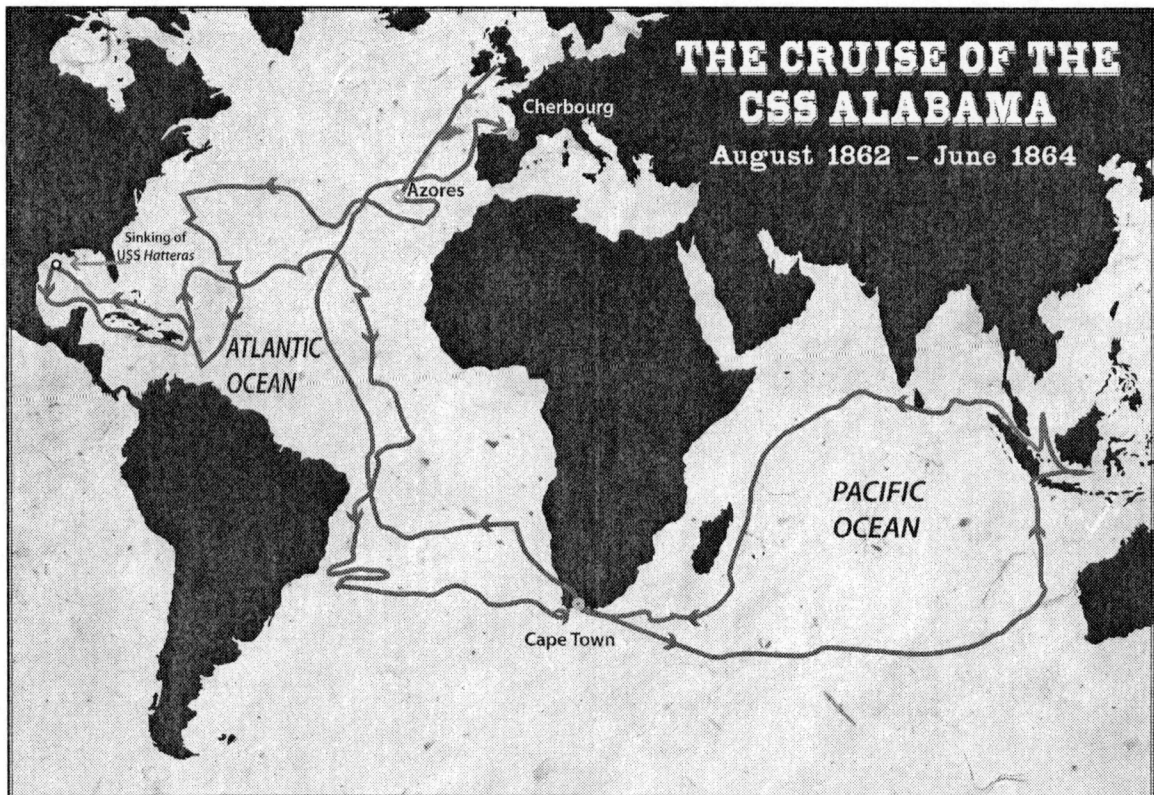

THE CRUISE OF THE CSS ALABAMA
August 1862 – June 1864

Cherbourg
Azores
Sinking of USS Hatteras
ATLANTIC OCEAN
PACIFIC OCEAN
Cape Town

This painting of the CSS *Alabama* was created by J. W. Schmidt.

took 29 prizes while raiding the busy shipping lanes off the coast of Brazil. On May 3rd, the *Alabama* captured the *Sea Lark*, its richest prize with various cargo valued at $550,000.

Prisoners reported unusual conditions on the *Alabama*. The captain of the *Amazonian* noted that there was no lack of want with cargo stacked everywhere. However, the ship and sailors were filthy and disordered like on a pirate ship.

As the the reputation of the *Alabama* grew, merchant ships avoided major shipping lanes while the U.S. Navy closed in. Semmes headed toward Africa, arriving in Cape Town, South Africa, on August 5, 1863. A crowd waiting to greet the *Alabama* witnessed her capture of the *Sea Bride* just off the coast. Crewmembers were greeted as heroes in South Cape as thousands flocked to tour the infamous raider. That same year, Richmond journalist Edward C. Bruce wrote:

> She bears the name of a noble State, and sooth
> she bears it well.
> To us she hath made it a word of pride, to the
> Northern ear a knell.
> To the Puritan in the busy mart, the Puritan on
> his deck,
> With "Alabama" visions start of ruin, woe, and
> wreck.

In September 1863, the *Alabama* began a 4500-mile cruise across the Indian Ocean. After going three months without a capture, Semmes took three prizes near Indonesia and the Strait of Malacca while evading the USS *Wyoming*. Semmes learned from old newspapers about Confederate defeats at Gettysburg and Vicksburg but remained undaunted.

Semmes stopped at the French island of Condore before receiving a grand reception at Singapore. There, he saw 22 Yankee ships moored and too afraid to venture out. The *Alabama* left Singapore on the day before Christmas 1863 and returned to Cape Town. There, Semmes read more bad news about Confederate setbacks. The *Alabama* briefly returned to Brazil, capturing two more Yankee ships before heading to France for much-needed repairs. By this point, the copper coverings on the bottom of the ship were peeling off, the keel was leaking, and timber beams were splitting.

The *Alabama* arrived at Cherbourg, France on June 11, 1864. The armor-clad USS *Kearsarge* under Semmes' former bunkmate Captain Winslow arrived three days later, preventing Semmes' escape. Unable to do much to repair his ship, Semmes decided to fight rather than rot in the harbor.

Captain Raphael Semmes stands on the deck of the raider CSS *Alabama*.

On June 19th, the *Alabama* steamed out to meet the *Kearsarge*. The two ships circled seven times as they exchanged fire. The *Alabama* was no match for the well-drilled men of the *Kearsarge* and her two 11-inch Dahlgren guns. The *Alabama's* fuses and powder were in bad shape after two years at sea, and many of her shells failed to explode. The *Alabama* sank after about 70 minutes of battle. Semmes and 41 of his crew were rescued by sympathetic Englishman John Lancaster's steam yacht, the *Deerhound*. In her brief two-year odyssey, the *Alabama* had collected 65 prizes and over 2000 prisoners, making her arguably the greatest raider in naval history

John Winslow

Semmes made his way back to Texas via Mexico and then to Richmond. He commanded the James River Squadron during the final months of the war and surrendered along with Joseph E. Johnston's army in late April 1865. Semmes was charged with treason, but the charges were eventually dropped. In his later years, he worked as a professor, county judge, and newspaper editor before returning to private law practice in Mobile.

The USS *Kearsarge* was a *Mohican*-class sloop-of-war armed with two 11 inch Dahlgren guns, four 32-pounder guns, and one 30-pounder Parrott rifle.

U.S. NAVAL HISTORICAL CENTER

CSS SHENANDOAH

The raider CSS *Shenandoah* has the distinction of instigating the final acts of aggression during the Civil War. A former cargo ship, the *Shenandoah* set sail from England to the Bering Sea in the northern Pacific under the command of Captain James I. Waddell. She captured 38 prizes, most of which were Yankee whaling ships working near the Aleutian Islands.

On June 27th, Captain Waddell learned from a newspaper that Lee had surrendered two months before. A week later he learned that the war had ended. Fearing possible charges of treason, Wadell altered the *Shenandoah* to look like a commerce ship and crossed the Pacific and Atlantic Oceans while avoiding pursuing U.S. ships. Arriving in Liverpool on November 6, 1865, the last Rebels surrendered to the British.

Semmes published his *Memoirs of Service Afloat During The War Between the States* in 1869, explaining and defending his view of the Lost Cause. He died in 1877 after contracting food poisoning from eating shrimp and was buried in Mobile. The wreck of the *Alabama* was found in 1984, and many artifacts have since been recovered including the ship's bell, cannons, tableware, and even commodes.

PHILADELPHIA MUSEUM OF ART

French artist Édouard Manet created this impressionistic painting of the battle between the CSS *Alabama* and the USS *Kearsarge*.

Philip Henry Sheridan

Union General
Born: March 6, 1831
Died: August 5, 1888

Philip Henry Sheridan was one of the war's most courageous men and, at times, one of the most ruthless. Lincoln once unflatteringly described him as "a brown, chunky little chap, with a long body, short legs, [and] not enough neck to hang him..." Sheridan's men described him affectionately as Little Phil. By the end of the war, Sheridan had secured a place of honor almost equal to Ulysses S. Grant and William T. Sherman.

Sheridan was born in Albany, New York, but his parents moved to Perry County, Ohio, when he was still a young child. He received a basic education by attending a village school until age 14. He continued to read and gained a reputation as a historian. He helped settle arguments while working as a clerk and bookkeeper. Entering West Point at age 17, he was held back a year after attacking a fellow cadet. In 1853, he graduated near the bottom of his class.

First stationed in Texas on the Mexican border, Sheridan was later transferred to California to conduct topographical surveys. He experienced his first combat while leading small units against Native Americans in the Pacific Northwest

Sheridan was promoted to Captain shortly after the attack on Fort Sumter. He joined General Henry "Old Brains" Halleck's staff in the fall of 1861 at Jefferson Barracks, Missouri. After reconciling a financial crisis and impressing Halleck as a staff officer, Sheridan was promoted to quartermaster for the Army of Southwest Missouri.

He served under General Samuel Curtis at the Battle of Pea Ridge in March 1862. During that campaign, he showed character in uncovering a profiteering ring. Fellow officers were stealing horses from civilians and then demanding payment from Sheridan. He refused to pay out for the horses.

Sheridan used the influence of friends to secure a position as a Colonel leading the 2nd Michigan Cavalry. Though he had never led cavalry before, his leadership during the battle at Booneville, Mississippi, impressed his commander, General William Rosecrans. After the battle, he was promoted to major general. At about the same time, he was given a horse named Rienzi that he rode for the remainder of the war.

MATTHEW BRADY

Sheridan relaxed for this portrait by famous war photographer Matthew Brady.

In 1863, Sheridan's forces captured Missionary Ridge at the Battle of Chattanooga. This impressed Grant, who then chose him to command the Army of the Potomac's Cavalry Corps. This move brought Sheridan to the Eastern Theater. His forces participated in the 1864 Overland Campaign mostly as a reconnaissance force. It was during this time that Grant planned a special task for Sheridan.

THE SHENANDOAH VALLEY CAMPAIGN

On June 10, 1864, General Jubal Early led 10,000 Rebels out of the Shenandoah Valley on a raid near Washington, D.C. Though the raid caused more dismay than damage, it convinced Lincoln and Grant that it was time to eliminate the South's last center of strength. The Shenandoah Valley was a prime source of food and supplies for the Rebel armies. Grant wanted the valley turned into a "barren waste" and gave the job to Sheridan.

Jubal Early

Grant combined four commands to create the Middle Military Division and told Sheridan to destroy anything in the valley that he could not use. Sheridan embraced the mission, reportedly

SHENANDOAH VALLEY CAMPAIGN
August–October 1864

THURE DE THULSTRUP/L. PRANG & CO.

Philip Sheridan leads a charge during the Third Battle of Winchester. Sheridan's men inflicted heavy casualties during the battle.

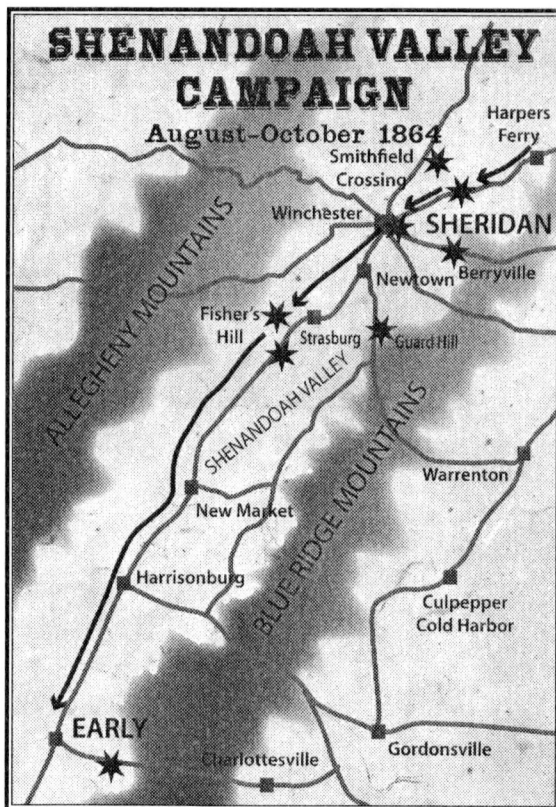

saying, "If a crow wants to fly down the Shenandoah, he must carry his provisions with him."

Sheridan spent six weeks sizing up the condition of Jubal's army. He made his move on September 19th, sending 37,000 Union soldiers against 15,000 Rebels at Winchester. Two Union divisions successfully conducted a classic saber charge, capturing almost 2000 prisoners. Smarting from the loss of one-fourth of his army at the Third Battle of Winchester, Early retreated to Fisher's Hill. Sheridan maintained pressure by attacking and defeating Early at Fisher's Hill three days later. Early retreated 60 miles back to a pass in the Blue Ridge Mountains.

BATTLE OF CEDAR CREEK

The Rebels were loathe to leave the Shenandoah Valley in the hands of the Yankees. Robert E. Lee reinforced Early with an infantry division

General Sheridan leads a charge in this Kurz & Allison print of the Battle of Cedar Creek.

and cavalry brigade. Early's 18,000 men surprised 30,000 Union soldiers with an early morning attack at Cedar Creek on October 19, 1864.

While the Union fled in disorder, Early's hungry men started foraging for food in the Union camps. Sheridan, returning from a conference in Washington, D.C., rode hard toward the battle. Strangely, his retreating troops met him with cheering. Sheridan rallied them, say-

TRIVIA

The systematic plundering of Loudoun County by Sheridan's men during Sheridan's Shenandoah Valley Campaign included:
- 3772 horses
- 10,918 beef cattle
- 15,000 swine
- 435,802 bushels of wheat
- 77,176 bushels of corn
- 12,000 pounds of bacon
- 71 flour mills
- 8 saw mills
- 1200 barns
- 947 miles of rail
- 1 train depot

ing, "...don't cheer me! If you love your country, come up to the front!...There's lots of fight in you men yet." His men responded, and Sheridan turned defeat into a decisive victory. Early lost 3000 men and almost all of his artillery. Cedar Creek was the final major battle in the Shenandoah Valley Campaign.

Sheridan's victories in the Shenandoah Valley helped secure Lincoln's reelection against George B. McClellan several weeks later. In addition, the way was open to render 400 square miles of the Shenandoah Valley unusable to the South.

Though Early's force was eliminated as a threat, partisan cavalry continued to launch small spoiling attacks against Union forces. John S. Mosby led a particularly troublesome group of partisan cavalry called Mosby's Raiders (43rd Battalion, Virginia Cavalry). Sheridan responded in November 1864 by cleaning out Mosby's base of operations, Loudoun County. Sheridan wrote his former commander Henry Halleck, saying, "...I will soon commence on Loudoun County, and let them know there is a God in Israel." By this time, Halleck had risen to chief of staff in charge of the administration of all Union armies.

Mosby's Raiders were displaced, but they never officially surrendered. They simply disbanded after Lee's surrender at Appomattox Court House. Sheridan's actions gained him a hated reputation among Virginians, rivaling Sherman's in Georgia and South Carolina.

Sheridan's subordinate, George A. Custer, trapped and destroyed the remnants of Early's army in March 1865. Custer would later meet his demise against Plains Indians at the Battle of Little Bighorn. This development freed Sheridan's forces to join Grant in

George Custer

pursuing Lee. Sheridan personally led an assault at Five Forks on April 1, 1865. The assault broke the stalemate and set the stage the next day for

THE PHOTOGRAPHIC HISTORY OF THE CIVIL WAR

General Sheridan relaxes while seated outside an army tent.

a Union breakthrough at Petersburg. Sheridan's forces subsequently blocked Lee at Appomattox, hastening his surrender.

SHERIDAN AFTER THE WAR

Considered a Union hero at war's end, Sheridan had a diverse and interesting post-war career. He was appointed governor of the Fifth Military District over Tennessee and Texas. President Andrew Johnson removed him for his tyrannical ways.

In 1867, Grant sent Sheridan out west to bring Indians onto reservations. Sheridan instituted a campaign of attacking winter camps and slaughtering bison to deprive the Indians of food.

The campaign was brutal but effective. Sheridan showed sympathy by demanding that Congress feed and care for the displaced and defeated Native Americans.

In 1871, Sheridan oversaw federal relief after the Great Chicago Fire. Marrying in 1875, his family lived in a house donated by grateful Chicagoans. He successfully lobbied to save Yellowstone National Park from developers in 1882. The next year, he was promoted to Commanding General of the U.S. Army. Sheridan died after suffering a series of heart attacks at age 57 in 1888. He was buried at Arlington National Cemetery.

Sheridan's memory has been honored with his image on currency, postage stamps, and bronze statues. Countless streets, counties, schools, and even a tank—the M551 Sheridan—bear his name. Thomas Buchanan Read wrote a famous poem , "Sheridan's Ride," about the Union hero's role in the 1864 Battle of Cedar Creek.

Hurrah! hurrah for Sheridan!
Hurrah! hurrah for horse and man!
And when their statues are placed on high,
Under the dome of the Union sky,
The American soldier's Temple of Fame;
There with the glorious general's name,
Be it said, in letters both bold and bright,
"Here is the steed that saved the day,
By carrying Sheridan into the fight,
From Winchester, twenty miles away!"

Joshua Lawrence Chamberlain

Union General
Born: September 8, 1828
Died: February 24, 1914

The accomplishments of Famous Man Joshua Lawrence Chamberlain were little-celebrated until the late 20th Century. At that time, books, movies, and a high-profile documentary boosted his legacy. A school teacher when the southern states seceded, Chamberlain rose to become a decorated warrior who played an important role in bringing the war to an end.

Joshua, the oldest of five children, was born and raised in Brewer, Maine. His parents named him after sea captain James Lawrence, who famously quipped, "Don't give up the ship!" Chamberlain loved the outdoors. He held the military in great esteem due to his ancestor's participation in the American Revolution and the War of 1812.

An extraordinary student, Chamberlain eventually achieved fluency in at least nine languages. He attended Bowdoin College where one of his professors was Calvin Stowe, the husband of Harriet Beecher Stowe. After graduation, he attended Bangor Theological Seminary. In 1855, he returned to Bowdoin and joined the faculty as professor of rhetoric and languages.

A QUICK LEARNER

Chamberlain could have spent the war safe in his classroom far from the front lines. He was even offered a leave of absence to study abroad in Europe. However, Joshua felt that he had a moral responsibility to defend his nation and fight slavery. He left the classroom and joined the army.

The 20th Maine formed with 1621 men after President Lincoln's second call for troops. By the time the regiment arrived at Gettysburg, just 266 men would remain. Chamberlain was appointed Lieutenant Colonel of the 20th under Colonel Adelbert Ames.

Chamberlain applied his keen study skills to quickly learn tactics. The unit participated in several of the war's most influential battles. It served as a reserve unit at Antietam. At Fredericksburg, the regiment suffered heavy casualties assaulting Marye's Heights. Survivors were forced to spend a night on the open field below the Heights by sheltering behind the bodies of dead comrades.

Adelbert Ames

In May 1863, Chamberlain assumed command of the Maine 20th. Shortly before the Battle of Gettysburg in early July, Colonel Chamberlain was given responsibility of 120 men of the Maine 2nd. The soldiers had mutinied after many of their comrades' enlistments ended and the regiment disbanded. Chamberlain was told

JOHN MCKEAN

The regimental flag of the 20th Maine featured an eagle on a dark blue field.

A 1909 photograph shows Little Round Top (left) and Big Round Top (right) as they appeared from the perspective of advancing Rebels.

that he could shoot the men if necessary. Instead, he persuaded all but a few men to fight in the upcoming battle.

GETTYSBURG

On the second day of battle at Gettysburg, the Army of the Potomac's commander George Meade sent General Gouverneur Warren to scout the southern end of the Union lines. He found Little Round Top completely unguarded. If the Rebels seized it, it could be a strong point from which to roll up the Union flank.

The 44th New York, 16th Michigan, 83rd Pennsylvania, and 20th Maine were dispatched in haste to hold the strategic ground. Colonel Strong Vincent placed the 20th Maine, along with Major Homer Stoughton's 2nd U.S. Sharpshooters, at the far left of the line. Vincent told Chamberlain to hold at all costs

Confederate General John Bell Hood's Texas regiments attacked the center of Vincent's line. Only a rally by the 140th New York Zouaves prevented the 20th Maine from being cut off. Meanwhile, Chamberlain arranged his men in a right angle to prevent a Rebel flanking maneuver. They succeeded in repulsing determined charges by two Alabama regiments. Color Sergeant Andrew J. Tozier of the former Maine 2nd stood heroically defending the regiment's flag, inspiring the men during the desperate struggle.

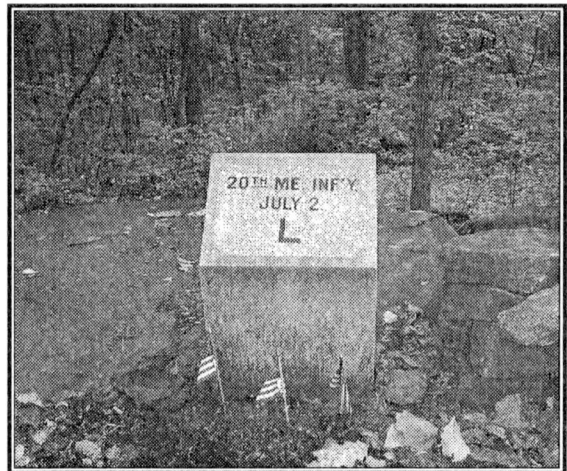

A marker shows the far left position of the Union line on Little Round Top held by the 20th Maine Regiment during the Battle of Gettysburg.

After running out of ammo, Chamberlain ordered his men to fix bayonets. He then led a charge down the hill. The regiment hesitated a moment before surging forward and sweeping the surprised Alabamians off of Little Round Top. During the charge, Chamberlain was almost killed when a rebel officer held a pistol to his face and pulled the trigger. The pistol misfired. Strong Vincent was not so fortunate; he was killed during the battle.

The unexpected countercharge preserved the Union's position on day two and encouraged

The Confederate defenses at Petersburg, abandoned in April 1865, reflect a sophistication unknown at the beginning of the war. These well-built trenches would not have looked out of place on the Western Front during World War I.

A Union siege mortar nicknamed the "Dictator" was brought in by rail to attempt to break General Lee's lines at Petersburg.

Robert E. Lee to order the ill-advised Pickett's Charge against the Union center the next day. Wounded twice during the battle, Chamberlain earned the nickname of Lion of Little Round Top in addition to earning a Medal of Honor.

APPOMATTOX COURT HOUSE

Chamberlain was wounded again in June 1864 at Petersburg. In November, the school teacher was promoted to brigadier general. He rejoined his unit in the final days of the Petersburg Campaign and was wounded one final time during the Battle of Five Forks. He remained with his unit and joined the pursuit of Lee's army.

On April 7, 1865, Ulysses S. Grant sent Lee a letter demanding surrender of the Army of Northern Virginia (AoNV). Lee refused. Two days later, he made one final attack against the much larger Union forces at Appomattox Station. When the attack failed, Lee realized, "There is nothing left for me to do but to go see General Grant, and I would rather die a thousand deaths."

At 4 pm on April 9th, 1865, Lee surrendered the AoNV at Wilmer McLean's house in the village of Appomattox Court House. McLean lived at Manassas when the war began. When his home was damaged during the Battle of First Bull Run, he moved to Appomattox Court House in the hope of avoiding the fighting.

Wilmer McLean

Lee appeared at the surrender in a full dress uniform, while Grant wore a private's blouse along with muddied pants and boots. Grant offered generous terms. Lee's men were allowed to return home and were offered immunity against treason as long as they obeyed U.S. laws. Grant allowed them to take their horses "...to put in a crop to carry themselves and their families through the next winter."

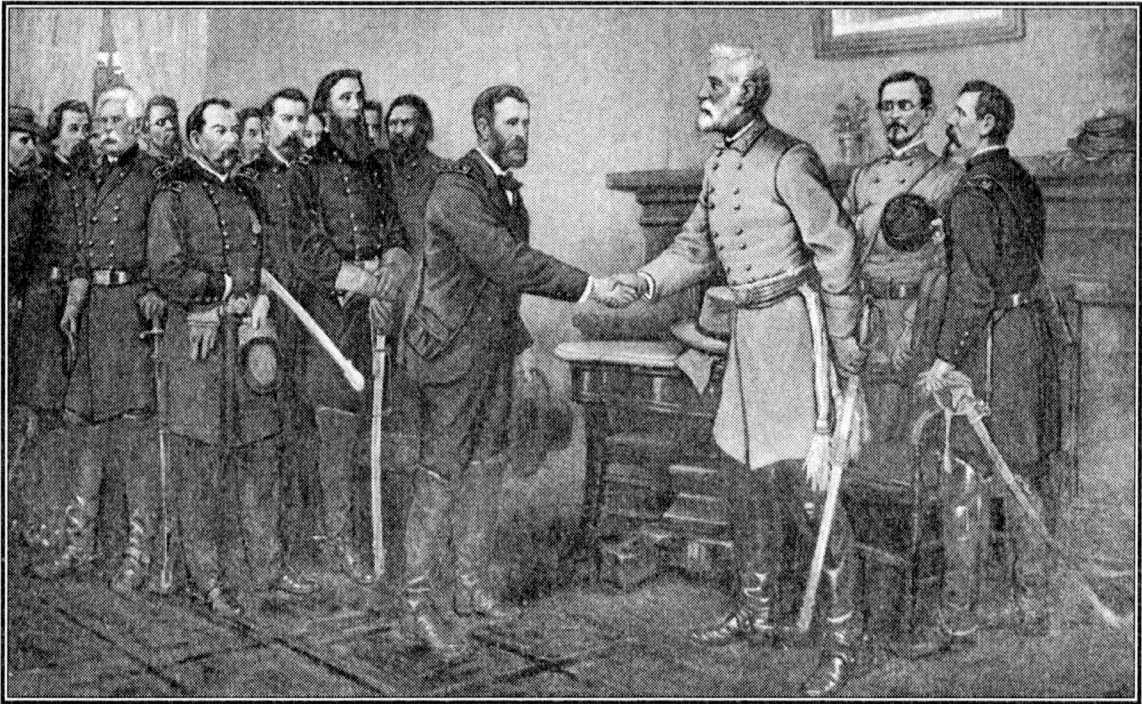

THOMAS NAST

Ulysses S. Grant and Robert E. Lee shake hands in the parlor of the McLean House at Appomattox Court House after signing the documents surrendering Lee's Army of Northern Virginia.

After signing the surrender documents, Lee shook hands with all of Grant's officers. Grant and Lee saluted and departed. News of the surrender ignited cheering in the Union camps, which Grant quickly ended by saying, "The rebels are our countrymen again." Grant also immediately sent three days' rations to Lee's famished men.

On April 12, 1865, Joshua Chamberlain was given the privilege of receiving the surrender of arms and flags from the AoNV. John B. Gordon led the Stonewall Brigade, reduced to 210 men after four years of struggle, at the head of the Rebel procession. Instead of gloating over the defeated foe, Chamberlain ordered his men to salute the men of the Stonewall Brigade and the rest of the AoNV as they passed by. Chamberlain described his thoughts on seeing the Confederate soldiers that day:

"Before us in proud humiliation stood the embodiment of manhood: men whom neither toils and sufferings, nor the fact of death, nor disaster, nor hopelessness could bend from their resolve; standing before us now, thin, worn, and famished, but erect, and with eyes looking level into ours, waking memories that bound us together as no other bond. Was not such manhood to be welcomed back into a Union so tested and assured?"

People crowded into streets in New York City and Washington, D.C., when they received news of the surrender. Washington, D.C., fired a 500-gun salute. Surprisingly, this was restrained compared to the 900-gun salute given after the fall of Richmond. Lincoln gave a speech on April 11th from the White House balcony. It would be several weeks more before all Confederate armies surrendered, but victory was assured.

RETURN TO SCHOOL

Chamberlain returned to his classroom at Bowdoin for a short stint the next year as a changed man. Grateful citizens elected him to four one-year terms as governor (1867-1871). He then returned once more to Bowdoin College where he served as president until 1883. He left Bowdoin for treatment of his minié-ball injury from Petersburg.

Over the years, Chamberlain wrote and spoke extensively about the war. He dabbled in business, including land speculation in Florida. He lived long after many of his fellow officers. His death in 1914 was attributed to the wound suffered at Petersburg 50 years previously. He is generally believed to be the last soldier to die of a Civil War wound. He was buried in Brunswick, Maine.

WIKIPEDIA

The Chamberlain house in Brunswick, Maine is well maintained by the Pejepscot Historical Society.

Today, Chamberlain's home is a museum across the street from the campus of Bowdoin College. There, one can see the minié ball from Petersburg that contributed to the death of this Famous Man.

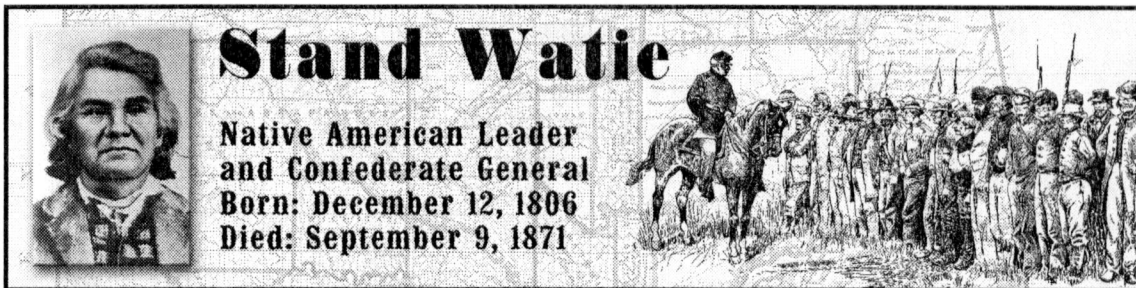

Stand Watie

Native American Leader and Confederate General
Born: December 12, 1806
Died: September 9, 1871

Sixty years before the United States extended citizenship to Native Americans, their ancestors played important roles during the Civil War. Stand Watie was a prominent Native American leader during the war. Born in the Cherokee Nation near Rome, Georgia, he was the son of a full-blooded Cherokee father and a half-Cherokee mother.

He was given the Cherokee name Degadoga, meaning "he stands." He was renamed Isaac S. Watie when his father joined the Moravian Church. When Degadoga reached adulthood, he chose to combine the English version of his Indian name, Stand, with his Moravian name, Watie.

DIVIDED IN PEACE AND WAR

Stand Watie signed the unpopular Treaty of New Echota in 1835 agreeing to removal of the Cherokee from Georgia. Most Cherokees placed partial blame on him for the Trail of Tears. When the Cherokee were forcibly relocated to the Indian Territory (Oklahoma), Watie settled at Honey Creek. In 1839, his uncle, cousin, and brother were ambushed and killed as the penalty under blood law for surrendering Cherokee land. Watie only escaped execution because he received a warning ahead of time.

The Civil War divided the Five Civilized Tribes. Some fought for the Union, but most fought for the Confederacy. The Native Americans did not have same respect for King Cotton as Southerners. They pledged support to the Confederacy in the hope that the Confederacy would grant them self-rule.

Watie accepted a commission as a Colonel and raised the 2nd Regiment of Cherokee Mounted Volunteers in 1861. The regiment included Indian troops from all of the Five Civilized Tribes: Cherokee, Chickasaw, Choctaw, Creek, and Seminole. They excelled as scouts and sharpshooters.

EARLY BATTLES

In December of 1861, Watie participated in the Battle of Chustenahlah. Confederate forces routed pro-Union Native Americans. As a result, 9000 Native Americans were forced to flee to Kansas in the dead of winter. An estimated 2000 died of exposure during what is remembered as the Trail of Blood on Ice.

In early 1862, the 1st and 2nd Cherokee Regiments fought under Confederate General Albert Pike at Pea Ridge, Arkansas. The Cherokee regiments engaged Union forces near Leeville, on the

Albert Pike

western edge of the battlefield. They fought bravely but recklessly as detailed in Pike's after-battle report:

> *"My whole command consisted of about 1000 men, all Indians except one squadron. The enemy opened fire into the woods where we were, the fence in front of us was thrown down, and the Indians charged full in front through the woods and into the open grounds with loud yells, took the battery, fired upon and pursued the enemy retreating through the fenced field on our right, and held the battery..."*

After the battle, Watie's 2nd Regiment was reorganized as the 1st Regiment.

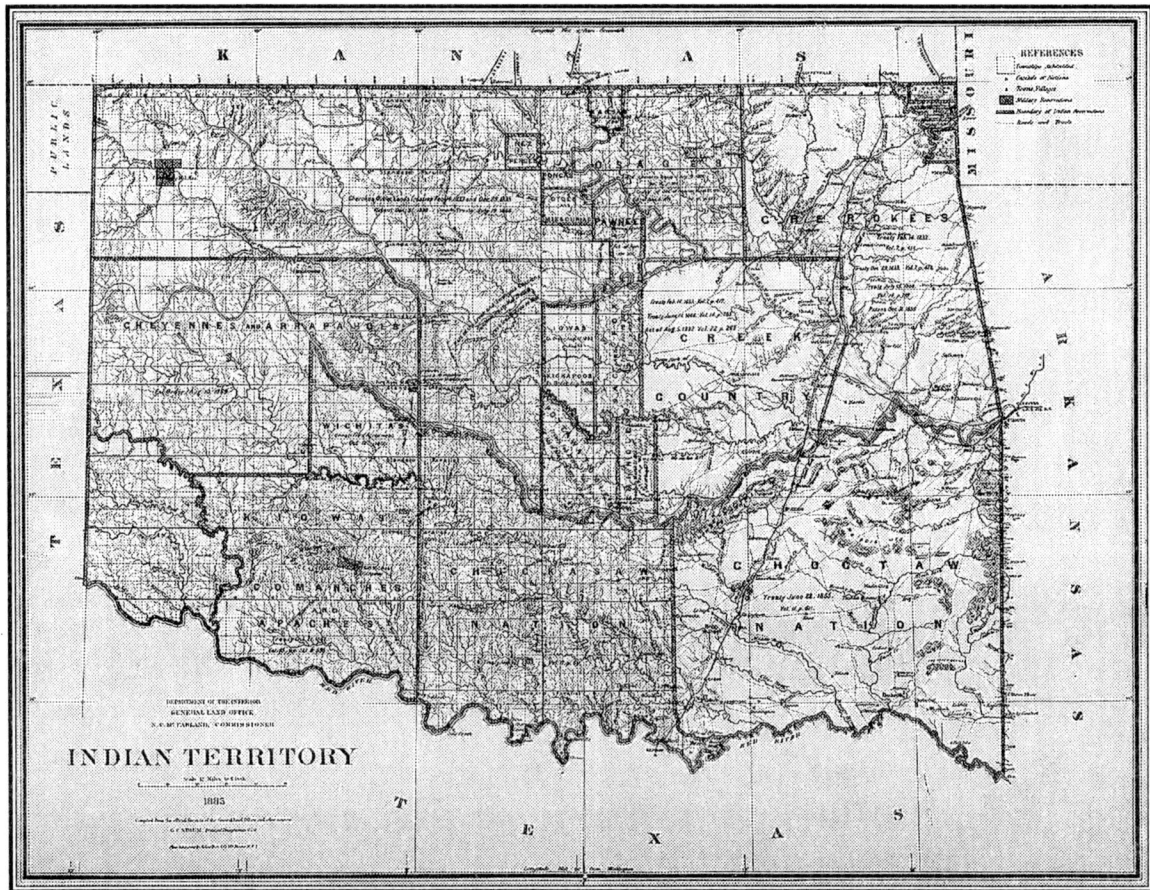

An 1885 map of the Indian Territory—modern day Oklahoma—graphically shows how land was divided between Native American tribes relocated to the region.

THE STRUGGLE FOR THE INDIAN TERRITORY

A series of battles in July 1863 left the Union in firm control of the Indian Territory. On July 1, Watie's 1st Regiment attempted to capture a Federal supply wagon train on its way down the Texas Road to Fort Gibson. The fort guarded the junction of the Arkansas River and Texas Road. Whoever held it controlled the two major paths of travel through the Indian Territory. Watie's troops were driven away by Union artillery fire while trying to hold a ford in Cabin Creek.

Confederate leaders responded by assembling 5700 Confederate troops at Honey Springs Depot under General Douglas Cooper. Their goal was to retake Fort Gibson. General James Blunt led 3000 Union troops south out of Fort Gibson to disrupt the buildup. On July 17th, the two sides met at Honey Springs.

The Battle of Honey Springs featured some of the most diverse forces to participate during the war. Union forces included the 1st Kansas Volunteer Infantry Regiment (black soldiers) and three regiments of the Indian Home Guard. These units consisted of Creek, Delaware, Kickapoo, Seneca, Shawnee, Quapaw, Osage, and

The pathway marks the position of the Union Line when the Battle of Honey Springs began.

Cherokee companies all fighting to reclaim their homelands. Confederate forces included Creek and Cherokee regiments. In fact, more Indian and black troops were involved in the battle than white troops.

General Cooper deployed the 20th and 29th Texas Cavalry and Texas Rangers along the Texas Road defending a crossing point along Elk Creek. The 1st and 2nd Creek Regiments held the left flank while the 1st and 2nd Cherokee under Watie formed the right wing.

Several Union assaults were repulsed before the Texas troops misunderstanding a Union call to move forward as a call to retreat, charged. The 1st Kansas broke the Texans' charge, creating a hole in the line. Cooper called a retreat. The Indian regiments fought bravely, ensuring an orderly retreat, but could not compete with Union soldiers armed with Sharps rifles. The rifles were accurate, long-range, and easy to reload even while riding on a horse. The Feder-

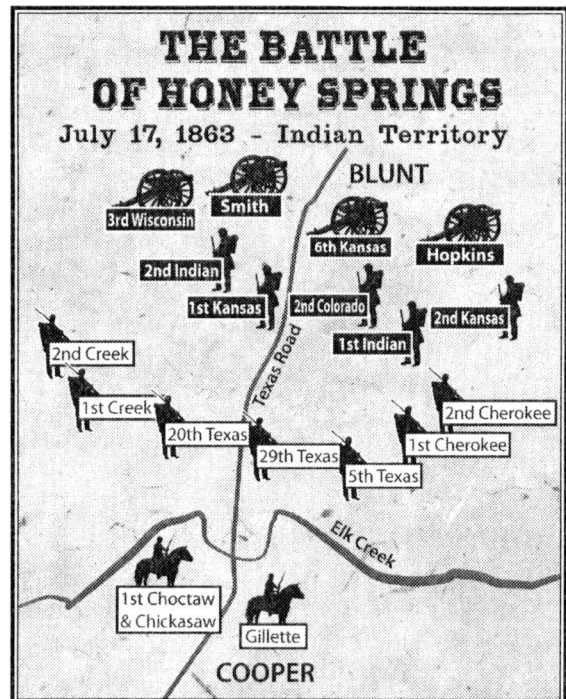

THE BATTLE OF HONEY SPRINGS
July 17, 1863 - Indian Territory

Stand Watie poses for a formal photograph.

als captured Honey Springs Depot, which the Rebels had set on fire while retreating.

In June 1864, Watie's men captured the Union steamboat *J.R. Williams* on the Arkansas River in Oklahoma Territory by forcing it to run aground. They captured $120,000 worth of goods including 150 barrels of flour and 16,000 pounds of bacon. Choctaws, Chicka-saws, Creeks, and Seminoles participated in the raid. It was the most decisive battle in the Indian Territory, though it did little to change the strategic situation.

On September 19, 1864, Watie and General Richard Gano led a night attack on a Federal wagon train to Fort Gibson. During the Second Battle of Cabin Creek, the Rebels captured 130 wagons and supplies. It was the last major battle in the Indian Territory.

CARRYING ON THE FIGHT

The surrender of Confederate armies in the Eastern Theater quickly followed Robert E. Lee's surrender in April 1865. General Richard Taylor in Mobile surrendered the last Confederate army east of the Mississippi River on May 8th. Meanwhile, several western Rebel armies continued the futile struggle.

The final battle of the war took place at Palmito Ranch in Texas on May 12-13, 1865. Brownsville was a point of conflict as supplies could enter Texas from Mexican ports just south of the border. Union General Lew Wallace negotiated an informal truce with the Confederates in March 1865 after the outcome of the war became apparent. For reasons that are still debated today, Union Colonel Theodore H. Barrett advanced on Brownsville more than a

The battlefield at Palmito Ranch has changed little since 1865.

month after the surrender at Appomattox. He had a diverse force consisting of black soldiers, Indiana volunteers, and Texas cavalry composed of whites, Mexicans, and Indians.

On May 13, Barrett met a small Confederate force at Palmito Ranch near Galveston. Barrett's 500 men easily pushed 190 Rebels back across an open prairie. While the Union paused on a hill to rest and regroup, John S. "Rip" Ford arrived with 300 Texas cavalry and field artillery.

Theodore H. Barrett

Ford was a colorful character who had arrived in Texas several months after the Battle of San Jacinto (1836) and worked as a lawyer, doctor, and judge. He led a cavalry charge after a brief bombardment, routing the Union line. Ford said, "Boys, we have done finely, we will let well enough alone, and retire." Thus ended the last battle of the Civil War.

John S. "Rip" Ford

Federal officers arrived in Galveston a few days later to arrange a permanent truce. Ford disbanded his small army rather than surrender.

The Cherokee chiefs met in a high council on June 15th and agreed to surrender. Watie gained a distinction as the last Confederate general to surrender on June 23, 1865 at Doaksville in the Indian Territory..

Watie was one of only two native Americans to reach rank of general during the war. The other was Union general and Seneca Indian Ely S. Parker. After the war, Watie returned to his home, which had been burned down by Union soldiers. Living out his days rebuilding his farm, he died in September 1871 and was buried in Delaware County.

CIVIL WAR...IN NEW MEXICO?

The Confederacy had grand plans for the American West. First, it would enforce its claim on the Arizona Territory covering parts of modern day Arizona and New Mexico. It's forces would then sweep north into Colorado to capture gold and silver mines to finance the war. Ultimately, it would break the Union blockade by moving west and seizing ports in California.

The ambitious campaign started well when Confederate Brigadier General Henry H. Sibley captured Santa Fe and Albuquerque in March 1862. He sent about 300 Texas troops under Major Charles Pyron to block the flow of Union supplies to the region. To do this, Pyron needed to capture Glorieta Pass—in the Sangre de Cristo Mountains in present-day New Mexico.

Henry H. Sibley

On March 26th, Pyron's troops skirmished briefly with 400 Colorado infantry and U.S. Cavalry under Major John Chivington. Both sides received reinforcements over the next two days. On March 28th, 1100 Confederates and 900 Union troops clashed in the Battle of Glorieta Pass. Rebels under John P. Slough first held their line of battle near Pigeon's Ranch and then pushed the Union troops back from the pass.

The victory celebration ended in shock upon the Rebels returning to camp. Chivington's Union troops, guided by Hispanic Lieutenant Colonel Manuel Antonio Chaves of the 2nd New Mexico Volunteers, had managed to sneak around the Rebels. They succeeded in burning the Confederate supply train. Without supplies, the Rebels were compelled to retreat to Santa Fe. The Confederate plan was dead. The South would never again seriously challenge Federal control of the West.

Andrew Johnson

17th President of the United States
Born: December 29, 1808
Died: July 31, 1875

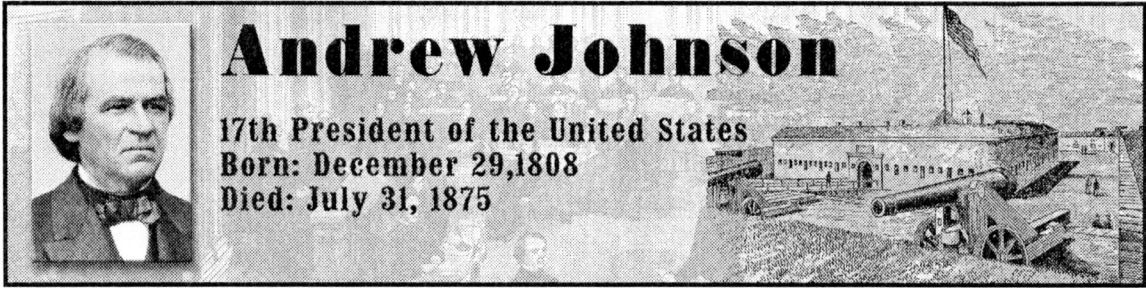

The end of fighting was not the end of the Civil War. Before the last soldier laid down his weapon, politicians began waging a long, bitter struggle to shape the future of the reunified nation. President Andrew Johnson was at the center of the struggle.

Born in 1808 in Raleigh, North Carolina, Johnson lived a childhood of poverty. His father died when Andrew was just three years old. The death was due to lingering effects of saving acquaintances from drowning. Receiving little education, Johnson was apprenticed to a tailor at 16 but soon ran away. He opened his own tailor shop in Greeneville, Tennessee.

Life began to improve for Johnson after he married in 1827. His wife helped him study, and he made it a habit to have people read to him while he worked. He enjoyed participating in debates in his shop and at a local academy. His speaking skills led to a political career built on stump speeches supporting the common man against the aristocracy.

First elected as an alderman in Greeneville, he quickly rose through the political ranks. He was elected to the U.S. House of Representatives (1843-1853), then as governor of Tennessee (1853-1857), and finally to the U.S. Senate (1857-1862).

Johnson remained in the Senate even after Tennessee seceded. As the only southern senator to remain loyal to the Union, this raised his profile in the North while angering Southerners. Abraham Lincoln appointed him the military governor of Tennessee in 1862. The state served as a laboratory in which to test Lincoln's ideas for reunifying the nation.

Though he was a Democrat, Republicans selected him as their candidate for Vice President in 1864. Lincoln and Johnson ran on the National Union Party ticket, a Republican derivative designed to attract war Democrats and border-state citizens who could not bring themselves to vote for a straight Republican ticket.

AN UNLIKELY PRESIDENT

Most vice-presidents serve their time in relative obscurity. This was not the case with Johnson. The assassination of Lincoln in March 1865 thrust Johnson into the turbulent Reconstruction period.

LIBRARY OF CONGRESS

Julian Vannerson took this portrait of Andrew Johnson in 1859.

Cabinet members look on as Chief Justice Salmon P. Chase swears in Andrew Johnson as President of the United States shortly after the death of Abraham Lincoln.

Johnson was a man with complex views. A southern Jacksonian Democrat who supported states' rights, he had remained loyal to a government asserting federal rights. He blamed southern slaveholders for instigating the Civil War. In 1864 he said, "Slavery is the cancer upon the body politic, which must be rooted out before perfect health can be restored." However, he also held contemporary southern views regarding race, saying, "This is a country for white men, and as long as I am president, it shall be a government for white men."

After Lincoln's death, he speedily brought the southern states back into the Union before Congress met in December. He said, "...there is no such thing as reconstruction. These states have not gone out of the Union, therefore reconstruction is unnecessary." Johnson described his plan in milder terms as Restoration. Southern states were allowed to reenter the Union by meeting three lenient terms:

1. Amnesty must be granted for Southerners swearing allegiance to the Union.

2. Only whites who swore loyalty and had been pardoned could vote in state constitutional conventions.

3. The Thirteenth Amendment abolishing slavery must be ratified.

The result was that states created governments mostly of old Confederate leaders. They promptly passed black codes limiting the rights of newly-freed African Americans. When Congress convened, it expressed displeasure with Johnson's approach and set about on a program known as Reconstruction that would punish the South.

The Reconstruction Congress was dominated by "Radical Republicans" led by Thaddeus Stevens and Benjamin Butler. They refused to seat any representative or senator with ties to the former Confederacy. Congress passed the Civil Rights Act of 1866 granting citizenship to blacks and forbidding discrimination through black codes. Johnson vetoed the Act, but Congress overrode it.

The Republicans sought to strengthen the Civil Rights Act of 1866 with a constitutional amendment. The Fourteenth Amendment—eventually adopted in 1868—granted legal and citizenship rights to all Americans. Johnson contested passage of the amendment, while it spurred race riots in the South. The amendment would be widely ignored in southern states.

Reconstruction created the opportunity for African Americans in southern states to attend school for the first time.

GRAND, NATIONAL UNION BANNER FOR 1864.
LIBERTY., UNION AND VICTORY.

A Currier & Ives print features Abraham Lincoln and Andrew Johnson as candidates on the National Union ticket during the 1864 presidential election.

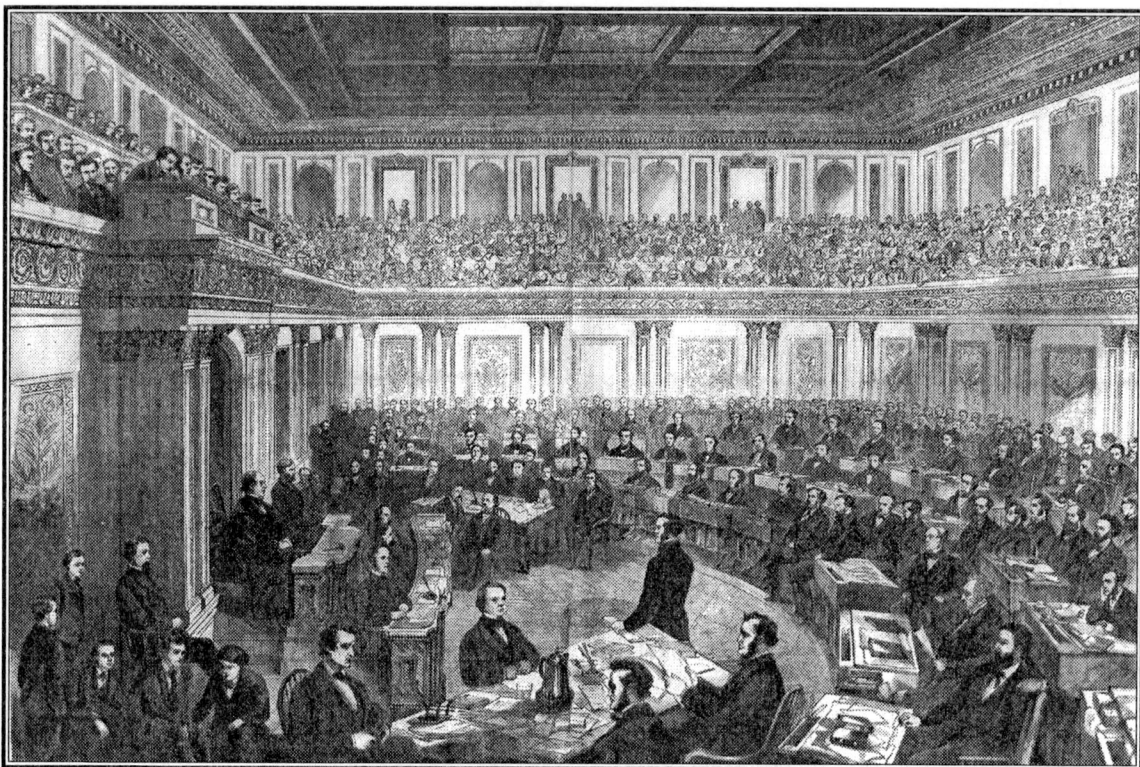

Chief Justice Salmon P. Chase presides over the Senate during the impeachment trial of Andrew Johnson.

Passage of the Fourteenth Amendment proved popular in northern states, propelling the Radicals to big wins in the midterm 1866 election. Believing that they had a mandate, Radicals placed southern states back under military rule, splitting southern states into five districts in March 1867. Under martial law, blacks could vote and run for office. As a result, many black delegates attended state constitutional conventions. Hundreds of African Americans held office at all levels of government during Reconstruction, including U.S. Senators Hiram Rhodes Revels and Blanche Bruce from Mississippi.

IMPEACHMENT

The battle between the Radical Congress and President Johnson intensified after the midterm elections. Johnson blocked the enforcement of laws and vetoed more bills than any previous President. The Radicals responded by passing laws restricting presidential powers, including the Tenure of Office Act. The law blocked Johnson from removing any official from office who had been confirmed by the Senate.

Johnson broke the Tenure of Office Act by dismissing Secretary of War Edwin M. Stanton and replacing him with General Lorenzo Thomas. Stanton barricaded himself in his office rather than go quietly. As a result, on February 24, 1868 the House of Representatives voted to impeach (remove) Johnson. The impeachment trial began in the Senate and lasted 11 weeks. A two-thirds vote was required to remove Johnson from office. The May 16th vote fell one vote short, 35 to 19, allowing Johnson to finish his term.

BRITTANICA

Scalawags were Southerners who supported Reconstruction. Carpetbaggers—one is depicted in this cartoon—were Northerners who packed their belongings in cheap carpet suitcases and moved to the South.

One week later, Republicans nominated Ulysses S. Grant as their candidate for the 1868 election. Johnson received less than one-third of the votes at the Democratic National Convention in July, losing to Horatio Seymour. Grant trounced Seymour in the fall election.

In 1875, Johnson returned briefly to the Senate—the only former President to ever do so—for a special session representing Tennessee. He died of a stroke while visiting his daughter later that year. Andrew was buried near Greeneville in a cemetery that today is Andrew Johnson National Cemetery.

Reconstruction continued without Johnson. In 1869, the Fifteenth Amendment ensured that voting could no longer be denied based on "race, color, or previous condition of servitude." While the amendment extended the vote to black males, it did not make voting an absolute right.

Grant's administration was full of corruption, thus weakening the influence of the Radi-cal Republicans. Passage of the Amnesty Act in 1872 pardoned most Confederates. This allowed Democrats to regain control of state governments. In 1876, Americans elected Republican Rutherford B. Hayes. He had no desire to fight the white southern Democratic governments. Instead, he withdrew federal troops from southern states, and Reconstruction ended in 1877.

IMPACT OF THE WAR

Retaining a strong hold of southern governments, Democrats began to erode the rights of blacks. Groups like the Ku Klux Klan used fear to intimidate blacks, and whites who supported them, from voting Republican. Southern states passed new constitutions effectively disenfranchising blacks and poor whites. Few blacks were allowed to serve in any official capacity.

Jim Crow laws segregated society and severely restricted the rights blacks had enjoyed under Reconstruction. The U.S. Supreme Court's *Plessy* v. *Ferguson* decision in 1896 cemented the legality of racial segregation for decades to follow. It was not until passage of the 1960s Civil Rights acts that all Americans in southern states were allowed to move about in society and vote on even terms. One product of Reconstruction, the Fourteenth Amendment, was key in helping African Americans argue for their rights.

The legacy of the Civil War is in a state of continual flux as evidenced today by the debate over use of the battle flag of Northern Virginia. Many Southerners view it as a symbol of pride and the southern way of life. Others view it and symbols such as commemorative statues, as archaic emblems of slavery and oppression.

The character of the South remains distinct from other regions even as its rural character has partially given way to industrialization. More than 150 years later, some Southerners still lament the Lost Cause and wonder how different life would be if the South had maintained its independence.

"Clara" Harlow Barton

Union Humanitarian
Born: December 25, 1821
Died: April 12, 1912

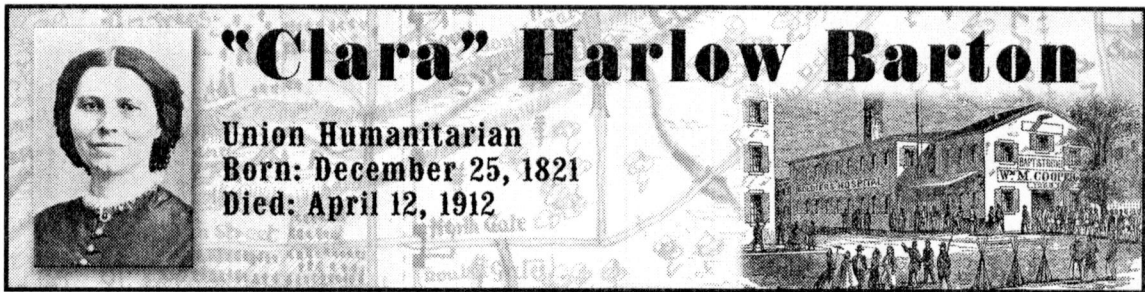

Clarissa "Clara" Harlowe Barton waited at a passenger station in Washington as a Baltimore and Ohio train delivered Union soldiers injured by a mob in Baltimore. The date was April 19, 1861, just seven days after the attack on Fort Sumter. Recognizing several of the soldiers as former schoolmates, Clara took the men to her sister's house. While caring for the wounded, Clara could not but help ponder how the "great national calamity" falling upon America would impact her future.

Clara's slender five-foot frame, dark brown hair, and beautiful face made her look much younger than her 39 years. The daughter of a veteran, Samuel Barton, Clara was unmarried by choice. A former schoolteacher, Clara had secured one of the first ever government jobs for women, serving as a clerk in the Patent Office. Clara had a gift of making people comfortable and willing to talk.

DETERMINED TO CONTRIBUTE

Clara was a strong believer in the Union cause and held a deep desire to join the Army, claiming, "The patriot blood of my father was warm in my veins." In the early days of the war, Clara struggled with how to help. Though restrained by the social belief that unmarried women did not belong on the battlefield, Clara was convinced her place was in the field, not behind the lines. A gifted writer, Clara wrote letters appealing for the donation of medical supplies, food, and other times to be distributed on the front lines.

In March 1862, from his deathbed, Clara's father encouraged her to take to the field. He told her that soldiers would respect a woman who respected herself. Clara finally felt free to "serve and

Soldiers wait for medical attention after the Battle of Chancellorsville.

Matthew Brady photographed Clara Barton in 1866.

Soldiers mill about an orderly Union field hospital at Brandy Station, Virginia.

sacrifice for my country in its peril and strengthen and comfort the brave men who stood for its defense." Clara wasted no time, following Ambrose Burnside's army as it attempted to meet up with John Pope's during the Seven Days' Battles.

Clara's first real test came during the Battle of Second Bull Run. After a disastrous defeat, thousands of wounded Union soldiers were carried eight miles to a rail junction. There, they were left exposed to the elements on rain-soaked hillsides until loaded on board a train. Clara, along with two other volunteers and a handful of surgeons, moved among the fallen men, nursing, feeding, and encouraging the dying men that "you must not give up."

Though she was already familiar with the horrors of warfare, it was not until the Battle of Antietam that Clara worked on the front line. In one incredible incident, a bullet ripped through her sleeve, hitting and killing a soldier Clara was tending. While working tirelessly at Antietam, Clara contracted typhoid fever. After recovering, she rejoined the Army of the Potomac only to have her hand become infected. She returned to Washington to recuperate.

In December 1862, Clara was present at the Union catastrophe at Fredericksburg. Shocked by the poor sanitation of field hospitals, she ordered her teams to perform basic sanitary jobs such as cleaning floors. Signs of improving medical care were apparent as ambulances whisked the wounded to a growing number of field hospitals.

In 1863, Clara's brother David was assigned to Port Royal, South Carolina. Clara accompanied him and assisted during several battles. On July 18th, Clara witnessed the brave but futile assault on Fort Wagner by Union forces, led by the 54th Massachusetts, a colored regiment. During her time on Morris island, Clara worked in a field hospital on the beach.

While at South Carolina, Barton wrote a friend, "I am singularly free, there are few to mourn for me, and I take my life in my hand and go where men fall and die, to see if perchance I can render some little comfort as the wife or mother would if she could be there."

On September 15th, General Quincy Gillmore informed Clara that her services were no longer required. Not knowing what to do next,

The volume of wounded soldiers overwhelms a Union field hospital after the Battle of Savage's Station.

depression enveloped Clara as she returned to Washington, D.C.

CLARA APPEALS TO THE NATION

Barton rushed to Fredericksburg after the Battle of Spotsylvania to help wounded diverted from field hospitals. Realizing her modest stock of supplies was inadequate, she wrote her first national appeal, citing "... the magnitude and intensity of suffering and want are so appalling as to wring from me a public call for aid."

As the end of the war drew near, Clara began assisting released POWs at a camp in Annapolis, Maryland. As a result of her growing national reputation, Clara received many letters from distraught women seeking informa-

tion about missing sons and husbands. Clara found new purpose in seeking out the fate of these men.

Clara attended President Lincoln's second inauguration on March 4, 1865, and deeply mourned his death six weeks later. The war over,

Ambulances of the 57th New York Regiment stand ready for action.

DANGEROUS HOSPITALS

No one anticipated the lengthiness of the Civil War and the magnitude of suffering that it would cause. Before the Battle of First Bull Run only one small hospital stood ready to receive the wounded. As it became apparent that the war would not end quickly, Union efforts to improve medical treatment gained momentum.

Technological advances led to weapons capable of inflicting appalling wounds. Minié-balls—conically-shaped iron and lead bullets—shattered bones as they sliced through human flesh. Grapeshot—small balls or pieces of metal loaded in canisters—fired by cannons shredded human bodies.

The terror for wounded soldiers only intensified in field hospitals. A lack of basic knowledge about sanitation, such as failing to clean instruments between treating patients, led to many unnecessary deaths. Hospitals were overcrowded and lacking in supplies and essential medicines. Diseases and infections ran rampant.

The establishment of the U.S. Sanitary Commission in 1861 was a significant step towards improving filthy and diseased military camps. Dorothea Dix's appointment to create a fledgling army nurses corps began to change attitudes towards women serving in field hospitals.

Jonathan Letterman, medical director for the Army of the Potomac, developed the first ambulance system to quickly evacuate wounded from the field. Decades before motorized vehicles, ambulances typically consisted of two men and a stretcher. After being carried wounded from the battlefield, patients might be brought directly to a field hospital or loaded on a horse-drawn cart for transportation.

Clara's work of accounting for the missing was just beginning.

ANDERSONVILLE PRISON

Dorence Atwater, an inmate at the Confederate prison in Andersonville, Georgia contacted Clara. Amazingly, Atwater had managed to keep and smuggle out a secret log containing names of over 12,000 prisoners who died at the squalid prison. In late 1865, Clara and Atwater traveled with an expedition to Andersonville to mark the graves. Unexpectedly, Clara had gained a reputation of honesty among African Americans. They came to her at Andersonville asking questions such as if Lincoln were really dead and if they were really free or not. In early 1866, a 74-page pamphlet, *A List of the Union Soldiers Buried at Andersonville*, was published, providing closure for many families.

Dorothea Dix

The publication of the Andersonville death registry convinced Congress to create the Office of Missing Soldiers headed by Clara. Over the next three years, Clara worked tirelessly to gather information, publish lists of missing soldiers,

LIBRARY OF CONGRESS

Captured Union soldiers wander around in the squalor of Andersonville Prison in Georgia.

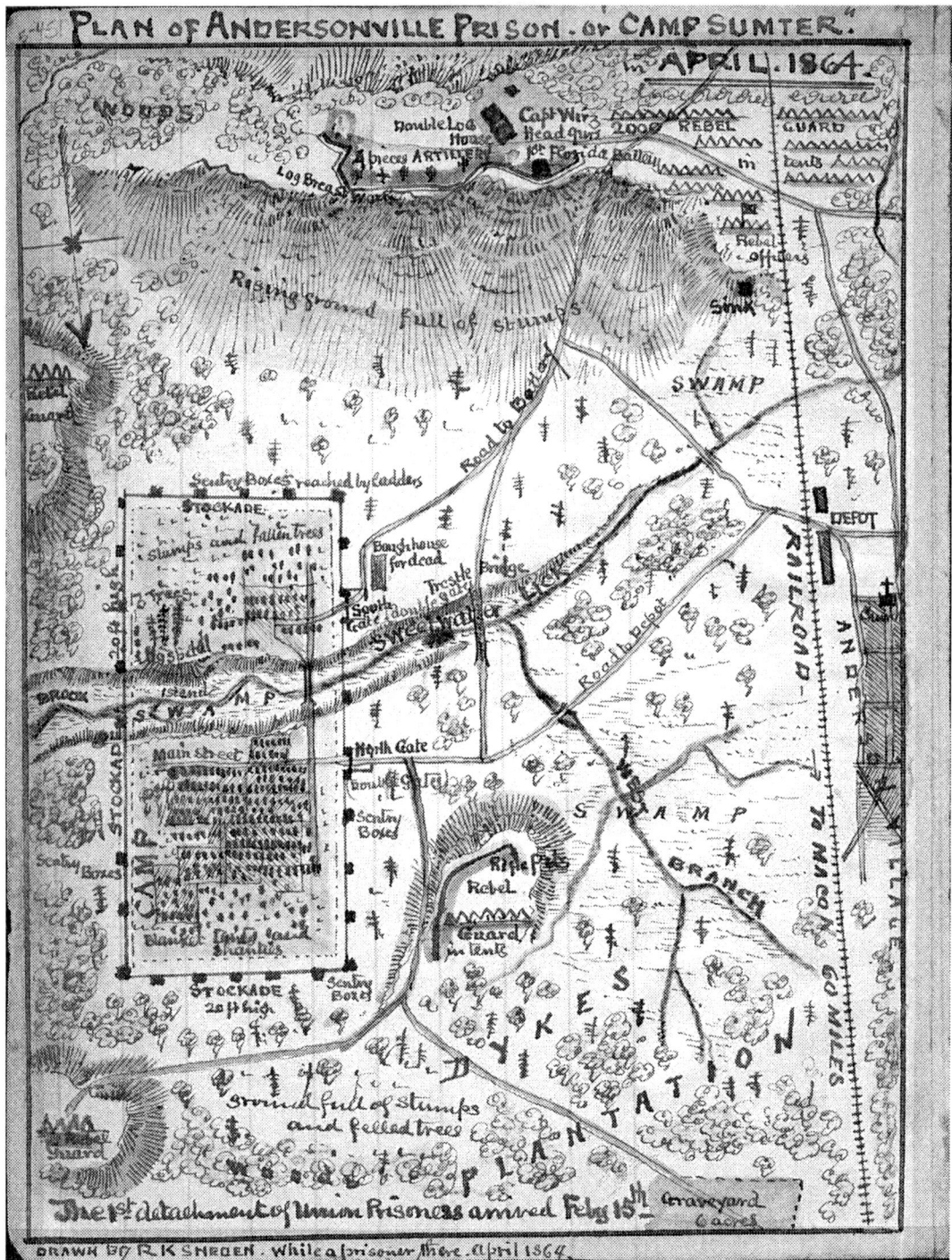

A Union prisoner drew this map while held captive at Andersonville prison in Georgia.

and correspond with anxious family members. In 1868, Clara, satisfied that everything possible had been done, sent a final report to Congress. More than 22,000 men had been identified. Sadly, more than 40,000 were never found.

Needing a steady income, Clara took advantage of her fame to embark on the lecture circuit. Her sincere, entertaining and informative style earned her wide acclaim as she crisscrossed the country. During this time, Clara also became involved with supporting women's suffrage and black civil rights.

In the 1870's, Clara campaigned for the creation of an American branch of the International Committee of the Red Cross. Her efforts were rewarded in 1881 when she was named the first president of the American Red Cross. In 1897, Clara sailed to Constantinople, opening a Red Cross headquarters in the middle of Turkey in response to the massacre of thousands of Armenians. The following year, the 77-year-old worked in hospitals in Cuba during the Spanish-American War. Clara's last field operation assisted victims of the Galveston hurricane in 1900.

Clara Barton died of tuberculosis in 1912 at the age of 90 in Glen Echo, Maryland. Her home at Glen Echo is today preserved as the Clara Barton National Historic Site. This Famous Woman's contributions toward soothing the suffering of others and advancing women's rights are her enduring legacy.

And thus we come to the end of Famous Men and Women of the Civil War. Hopefully, you now have a greater knowledge and appreciation for this tragic, but fascinating period of American history. Keep learning; there are many more Famous Men and Women in history for you to meet.

BIBLIOGRAPHY

GENERAL

Bishop, Chris & Ian Drury. *1400 Days: The Civil War Day by Day*. Gallery Books, 1990.

"Dueling." *Texas Escapes*. www.texasescapes. com/ClayCoppedge/Dueling.htm. Accessed January 23, 2016.

Gragg, Rod, ed. *The Illustrated Confederate Reader*. Gramercy Books: New York, 1989.

Holzer, Harold, Ed. *Hearts Touched by Fire: The Best of Battles and Leaders of the Civil War*. Random House: New York, 2011.

Hughes, Mark. *The New Civil War Handbook: Facts and Photos for Readers of All Ages*. Savis Beattie: New York, 2009.

"Impeachment of Andrew Johnson, The." *American Experience*. http://www.pbs.org/wgbh/ americanexperience/features/grant-impeach- ment/. Accessed June 10,2017.

Kennedy, Frances H., ed. *The Civil War Battlefield Guide*. Houghton Mifflin Company, 1990.

McPherson, James. *Battle Cry of Freedom*. Oxford University Press, 1988.

"Mexican War." *The Handbook of Texas*. tsha- online.org/handbook/online/articles/qdm02 Accessed November 1, 2015.

Oates, Stephen B. *The Approaching Fury: Voices of the Storm, 1820-1861*. Harper Collins Publishing: New York, 1997.

Rawls, Walton, ed. *Great Civil War Heroes and Their Battles*. Abbeville Press, 1985.

Stanchack, John. *Civil War*. Dorling Kinder- sly, 2000.

Swanson, James L. *Bloody Times: The Funeral of Abraham Lincoln and the Manhunt for Jefferson Davis*. Scholastic, Inc., 2011.

Weeks, Michael. *The Complete Civil War Road Trip Guide*. The Countryman Press: Woodstock, Vermont, 2009.

"Why Reconstruction Matters." *New York Times*. March 28, 2015. https://www.nytimes. com/2015/03/29/opinion/sunday/why-recon- struction-matters.html. Accessed June 19, 2017.

BIOGRAPHIES

"Albert Sidney Johnston." *Civil War Trust*. www. civilwar.org/education/history/biographies/ albert-johnston.html?referrer=https://www. google.com/. Accessed January 24, 2016.

Allen, Felicity. *Jefferson Davis: Unconquerable Heart*. University of Missouri Press: Columbia, 1999.

"Ambrose E. Burnside." *Civil War Trust*. http://www.civilwar.org/education/his- tory/biographies/ambrose-burnside. html?referrer=https://www.google.com/. Ac- cessed September 16. 2016.

"Andrew Johnson." *The White House*. https:// www.whitehouse.gov/1600/presidents/andrew- johnson. Accessed June 3, 2017.

"Andrew Johnson: History & Change." *National Park Service*. https://www.nps.gov/anjo/learn/his- toryculture/index.htm. Accessed June 10, 2017.

"Braxton Bragg." *Civil War Trust*. http://www. civilwar.org/education/history/biographies/ braxton-bragg.html?referrer=https://www. google.com/. Accessed January 6, 2017.

"Braxton Bragg: The Confederacy's Worst General." *Porter Briggs*. http://porterbriggs.com/braxton-bragg-the-confederacys-worst-general/. Accessed January 7, 2017.

Brookhiser, Richard. *Founder's Son: A Life of Abraham Lincoln*. Basic Books: New York, 2014.

"Chamberlain, Joshua." *National Park Service*. https://www.nps.gov/people/joshua-chamberlain.htm. Accessed Aroil 5, 2017.

Dabney, Robert Lewis. *Life and Campaigns of Lieutenant General Thomas J. Stonewall Jackson*. Sterling & Albright: 1865. Reprinted by Sprinkle Publications, 1983.

"David Dixon Porter." *Civil War Trust*. www.civilwar.org/education/history/biographies/david-porter.html?referrer=https://www.google.com/. Accessed August 31, 2016.

"Farragut, Admiral David Glasgow, Gravesite Bronx, New York." *National Park Service*. www.nps.gov/nr/travel/american_latino_heritage/Farragut_Gravesite.html. Accessed November 22, 2015.

"George B. McClellan." *Civil War Trust*. www.civilwar.org/education/history/biographies/george-mcclellan.html?referrer=https://www.google.com/. Accessed January 3, 2016.

"George H. Thomas (1816-1870)." *Encyclopedia of Virginia*. http://www.encyclopediavirginia.org/Thomas_George_H_1816-1870#start_entry. Accessed January 2, 2017.

Grant, Ulysses S. *Personal Memoirs of U. S. Grant*. Charles L. Webster & Co., 1894. Reprinted by Alacrity Press, 2012.

Grant, Ulysses S. & Meredith, Roy, ed. *Mr. Lincoln's General: U. S. Grant an Illustrated Biography*. Bonanza Books, 1959.

"James Longstreet." *Civil War Trust*. http://www.civilwar.org/education/history/biographies/james-longstreet.html?referrer=https://www.google.com/. Accessed September 10, 2016.

Johnson, Jr., Gregory, A. "T. J. 'Stonewall' Jackson." *Civil War Trust*. http://www.civilwar.org/education/history/biographies/thomas-jackson.html?referrer=https://www.google.com/ Accessed September 21, 2016.

"Joshua Lawrence Chamberlain." *Civil War Trust*. http://www.civilwar.org/education/history/biographies/joshua-lawrence-chamberlain.html?referrer=https://www.google.com/. Accessed March 19, 2017.

Lewis, Lloyd. *Sherman: Fighting Prophet*. Harcourt, Brace and Company, 1932.

Marrin, Albert. *Commander in Chief: Abraham Lincoln and the Civil War*. Dutton Children's Books: New York, 1997.

"Nathaniel Lyon." *Missouri Civil War Sesquicentennial*. mocivilwar150.com/history/figure/307. Accessed October 24, 2015.

"Nathan Bedford Forrest." *Civil War Trust*. http://www.civilwar.org/education/history/biographies/nathan-bedford-forrest.html. Accessed January 16, 2017.

"P.G.T. Beauregard." *Civil War Trust*. www.civilwar.org/education/history/biographies/p-g-t-beauregard.html?referrer=https://www.google.com/. Accessed August 7, 2015.

"Philip Sheridan." *Civil War Trust*. http://www.civilwar.org/education/history/biographies/phillip-sheridan.html?referrer=https://www.google.com/. Accessed March 15, 2017.

"Philip Sheridan" *Kansaspedia*. https://www.kshs.org/kansapedia/philip-sheridan/17323. Accessed April 16, 2017.

Reynolds, David S. *John Brown Abolitionist: The Man Who Killed Slavery, Sparked the Civil War, and Seeded Civil Rights.* Alfred A. Knopf: New York, 2006.

"Robert E. Lee." *Civil War Trust.* http://www.civilwar.org/education/history/biographies/robert-e-lee.html?referrer=https://www.google.com/. Accessed February 19, 2017.

Sawyer, Kem Knapp. *Harriet Tubman: A photographic Story of a Life.* DK Publishing: New York, 2010.

Sherman, William T. *Memoirs of William T. Sherman.* 2 vols. D. Appleton and Company, 1875. Reprinted by Alacrity Press, 2012.

"Stonewall Jackson's Last Days." *America's Civil War Magazine.* http://www.historynet.com/stonewall-jacksons-death.htm. Accessed November 23, 2016.

"Watie, Stand (1806-1871)." *Oklahoma Historical Society.* http://www.okhistory.org/publications/enc/entry.php?entry=WA040. Accessed May 9, 2017.

"Winfield Scott Hancock." *Pennsylvania Center for the Book.* http://pabook2.libraries.psu.edu/palitmap/bios/Hancock__Winfield_Scott.html

"Winfield Scott Hancock." *Civil War Trust.* http://www.civilwar.org/education/history/biographies/winfield-scott-hancock.html. Accessed January 13, 2017.

Eastern Theater

"Battles of Appomattox Station and Court House, The." *Civil War Trust.* http://www.civilwar.org/battlefields/appomattox-station/appomattox-station-history/the-battles-of-appomattox.html. Accessed February 19, 2017.

"Battle of Chancellorsville History." *National Park Service.* https://www.nps.gov/frsp/learn/historyculture/cvillehistory.htm. Accessed November 23, 2016.

"Battle of Five Forks, The." *Civil War Trust.* http://www.civilwar.org/battlefields/five-forks.html. Accessed February 19, 2017.

"Battle of Salem Church." *Civil War Trust.* http://www.civilwar.org/battlefields/chancellorsville/chancellorsville-history-articles/battle-of-salem-church-final.html. Accessed November 23, 2016.

"Defense of Little Round Top." *Civil War Trust.* http://www.civilwar.org/battlefields/gettysburg/gettysburg-history-articles/defense-of-little-round-top.html. Accessed April 30, 2017.

"Drewry's Bluff." *National Park Service.* www.nps.gov/rich/learn/historyculture/drewrys-bluff.htm. Accessed August 8, 2015.

"Fort Stedman." *Civil War Trust.* http://www.civilwar.org/battlefields/fortstedman.html. Accessed February 19, 2017.

"From the Stone Wall to a Shad Bake." *Emerging Civil War.* https://emergingcivilwar.com/2013/11/14/from-the-stonewall-to-a-shad-bake/. Accessed February 19, 2017.

O'Reilly, Frank. "The True Battle for Fredericksburg." *Civil War Trust.* http://www.civilwar.org/battlefields/fredericksburg/fredericksburg-history-articles/fredericksburgoreilly.html. Accessed September 19, 2016.

Rable, George C. "Fredericksburg." *Civil War Trust.* http://www.civilwar.org/battlefields/fredericksburg/fredericksburg-history-articles/fredericksburgrable.html. Accessed September 19. 2016.

"Seven Days Battles." *Civil War Trust.* www.civilwar.org/battlefields/seven-days-battles/?referrer=https://www.google.com/. Accessed December 27, 2015.

"10 Facts About the Petersburg Campaign." *Civil War Trust.* http://www.civilwar.org/battlefields/petersburg/10-facts-about-the-petersburg.html?referrer=https://www.google.com/. Accessed February 18, 2017.

"The Wilderness: Spotsylvania and Orange Counties, Virginia." *Civil War Trust.* http://www.civilwar.org/battlefields/the-wilderness.html?tab=facts. Accessed February 19, 2017.

WESTERN THEATER

"Benjamin Butler's Woman's Order." *Shotgun's Home of the American Civil War.* www.civilwarhome.com/butlerwomanorder.html. Accessed December 13, 2015.

"Camp Jackson Affair." *Missouri Civil War Sesquicentennial.* mocivilwar150.com/history/battle/168. Accessed October 24, 2015.

Castel, Albert. *General Sterling Price and the Civil War in the West.* LSU Press: Baton Rouge, 1993.

Groom, Winston. *Vicksburg, 1863.* Alfred A. Knopf, 2009.

"Confederates evacuate Corinth, Mississippi." *History.com.* www.history.com/this-day-in-history/confederates-evacuate-corinth-mississippi. Accessed August 23, 2015.

"Bleeding Kansas." *Kansaspedia.* www.kshs.org/kansapedia/bleeding-kansas/15145. Accessed August 1, 2015.

"Cherokees at Pea Ridge." *Civil War Trust.* https://www.civilwar.org/learn/articles/cherokees-pea-ridge. Accessed May 29, 2017.

"'Fetch up the Artillery' The Battle of Brice's Crossroads, June 10, 1864." *Civil War Trust.* http://www.civilwar.org/battlefields/bricescrossroads/brices-cross-roads-history/bricescrossroadshg.html. Accessed January 23, 2017.

"French Occupation of Mexico, The." *History 382: US Diplomatic History.* blogs.dickinson.edu/hist-382pinsker/2011/11/10/french-occupation-of-mexico-2/. Accessed August 28, 2016.

"Glorieta Pass." *Civil War Trust.* https://www.civilwar.org/learn/civil-war/battles/glorieta-pass. Accessed May 21, 2017.

Jones, Ralph. *The Battle of Honey Springs, Indian Territory, July 17, 1863.: Guide to the Interpretive Trails & Wayside Exhibits Text.* Oklahoma Historical Society, 2001.

"Johnston Surrenders at Bennett Place." *Civil War Trust.* http://www.civilwar.org/education/history/end-of-war/johnston-surrenders.html?referrer=https://www.google.com/. Accessed January 15, 2017.

Korn, Jerry. *The Civil War: War on the Mississippi, Grant's Vicksburg Campaign.* Time-Life Books, 1983.

"Mansfield." *Civil War Trust.* www.civilwar.org/battlefields/mansfield.html?tab=facts. Accessed August 28, 2016.

Missouri Department of Natural Resources, Division of Parks and Historic Preservation. *A State Divided: Missouri and the Civil War* (pamphlet).

National Park Service, *U.S. Department of the Interior. Pea Ridge* (pamphlet).

National Park Service, *U.S. Department of the Interior. Wilson's Creek* (pamphlet).

Nevin, David. *The Civil War: The Road to Shiloh, Early Battles in the West.* Time-Life Books, 1983.

"NM's role in 1862 battle lost in history." *Albuquerque Journal*. https://www.abqjournal.com/564212/nms-role-in-1862-battle-lost-in-history.html. Accessed May 21, 2017.

"Price's Missouri Raid of 1864." *The Civil War in Missouri*. www.civilwarmo.org/educators/resources/info-sheets/prices-missouri-raid-1864. Accessed October 17, 2015.

"Shiloh." Stacy D. Allen. *Blue & Gray Magazine: Civil War Sesquicentennial Edition*, 2010.

"Sterling Price (1809-1867)." *State Historical Society of Missouri Historic Missourian, The*. shs.umsystem.edu/historicmissourians/name/p/price/. Accessed October 4, 2015.

"Sterling Price." *Civil War Trust*. www.civilwar.org/education/history/biographies/sterling-price.html?referrer=https://www.google.com/. Accessed October 4, 2015.

Wheeler, Richard. *Sherman's March: An Eyewitness of the Cruel Campaign that Helped End the War*. Thomas Y. Crowell, 1978.

NAVAL

"10 Facts about the Battle of Hampton Roads." *Civil War Trust*. www.civilwar.org/battlefields/hampton-roads/hampton-roads-history/10-facts-about-hampton-roads.html Accessed September 15, 2015.

"CSS Shenandoah Surrenders." *Civil War Trust*. http://www.civilwar.org/education/history/end-of-war/shenandoah-surrenders.html. Accessed April 2, 2017.

"Damn the Torpedos! The Battle of Mobile Bay." *Civil War Trust*. www.civilwar.org/battlefields/mobilebay/mobile-bay-history-articles/damn-the-torpedoes-the.html?referrer=https://www.google.com/ Accessed November 29, 2015.

"David Dixon Porter." *National Park Service*. www.nps.gov/people/david-dixon-porter.htm Accessed August 26, 2016.

Fox, Steven. *Wolf of the Deep: Raphael Semmes and the Notorious Confederate Raider CSS Alabama*. Vintage Books: New York, 2007.

"Historic Mission, The." *Friends of the Hunley*. hunley.org/main_index.asp?CONTENT=MISSION Accessed November 1, 2015.

"Navy Runs the Guns At Vicksburg, April 16-17, 1863, The." *Naval History Blog*. https://www.navalhistory.org/2010/04/18/1045 Accessed September 1, 2016.

CONFEDERACY

Cannon, Jr., Devereaux. *The Flags of the Confederacy: An Illustrated History*. Pelican Publishing Company, 1994. Originally published by St. Luke's Press, 1988.

Thomas, Emory M. *The Confederate Nation: 1861-1865*. Harper Perennial: New York, 2011 edition with new introduction.

INDEX

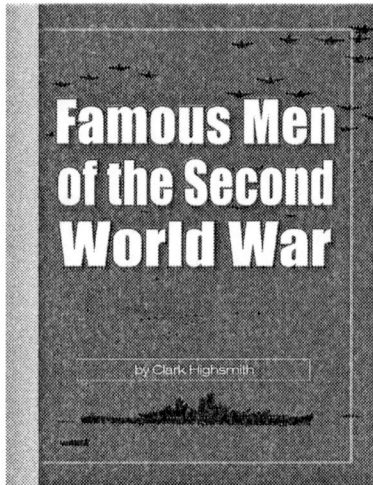